# women

## breaking through

# leadership

To: Susan

My best wishes for a sparkling future of love, joy, success and fun.

**Stefania Lucchetti**

**Anna Bisazza**

Stefania

Restless Travellers Publishing Limited

Sponsored by RTP Advisory (www.rtpadvisory.com)

printed on
recycled paper

**Restless Travellers Publishing Limited (RTP)**

Flat A, 6th Floor, Kin Luen Factory Building
89-91 Larch Street - Tai Kok Tsui, Kowloon
Hong Kong SAR

ISBN: 978-988-15108-1-5



Printed in China, January 2012

*To all the women who have contributed to creating a new world which thrives with opportunities and to my son Sky who will be a part of it* – Stefania

*To nonna and popo, my grandmothers and role models who with their strength, determination and femininity - plus a touch of irreverence - showed me that for a woman nothing is impossible* - Anna

# Contents

# Acknowledgments

First and foremost, the authors would like to thank Anson Chan, Deborah Kan, Christine Loh, Marie-Amelie Hoffman, Yana Peel, Catherine Bradley, Junko Nakagawa, Rainbow Pan, Connie Carnabuci, Angelina Kwan, Teresa Ko and Rachel Huf for their kindness in sharing their stories, thoughts and perspective with us.

A big thank you also goes to the team that worked behind the scenes: RTP's team and our editor Bong Miquiabas.

*Stefania* - A special thank you goes to Stefano, my husband, for his adventurous optimism and unwavering support. Your first reaction whenever I embark in a new project, no matter how ambitious and even if it is different from anything I have ever done before, is "go for it!", and so you did when I first talked to you about the idea of this book. As always, you have helped me keep the strength and determination to pursue this project, made sure I did not give up when I encountered difficulties, offered ideas and pointed out opportunities. Thank you.

*Anna* - My gratitude goes to Stefania for asking me to embark on this enlightening project. Thank you for believing in me and for stimulating my thoughts with your insightful and progressive views. A big thank you also goes to my friends and family, particularly Chika for listening to my endless monologues, and my mother for feeding me. Most of all I want to thank my husband, Cico. Without your support this project would have been twice as tough, especially since we found out I was expecting in the midst of it all. May the wisdom of the women in this book prepare our child - whether a boy or a girl, for a bright future ahead.

# Acknowledgments

[illegible]

# Introduction

When I was 34 years old, I hit a road bump. I had been a corporate lawyer for over 10 years. I had qualified in three jurisdictions sitting three long and exhausting bar exams (in Milan, in London and then again in Hong Kong). I had worked in top corporations and law firms in Europe and Southeast Asia. I was a highly skilled professional with an outstanding career path and at the same time I was enjoying good publishing success with my books.

At some point, however, my career as a lawyer, in the particular organization where I was then working, entered a strange chapter – it was a place where I could not see any future.

It happened more or less at a common time for many women, when I decided to get married and then have a baby. The intense pressure I experienced then, together with the downturn of the global economy which slowed down internal career prospects, prompted me to leave my job.

Certain for years that I would have a bright career, with no limits, I had done what most women do. I had studied and worked very hard at every stage of my life. I had relied on my technical competence. I always had a strong personality and often battled my bosses for personal space (having the liberty to go to the gym at lunchtime was one of the uphill battles I often fought in my early years, and sometimes even later) but I had always been a hard worker and I thought that would be enough to pull me through. But I made all the usual mistakes. I was one of those conscientious lawyers who didn't attend meetings I considered useless because I had more important work to do. When a male colleague, often younger than me, got a bigger office with a nicer view I didn't complain. I didn't put my foot down when a type A personality male colleague took the front line position in two deals where, actually, I was the one doing all the work.

In the end, the obvious thing happened. When I fell pregnant – and I was automatically excluded from any deal that mattered because I couldn't travel and I wasn't going to be available 24/7 for projects, I found myself losing all interest in the job.

In the meantime, my career as an independent consultant and writer took flight. I wrote my second book during my maternity leave and started getting some serious, very rewarding consulting engagements – including a teaching contract at the Hong Kong University of Science and Technology - during the same period. When I went back to the office after my maternity leave (my baby was three months old) and I was refused a request to work from home one day a week as a temporary flexible arrangement for those few months after going back to work - I lost all interest in continuing my career in that organization.

At the time, my choice felt natural and I took it as a special opportunity to get on the runway for an exciting entrepreneurial path while at the same time being more flexible to spend more time with my infant baby.

As time passed, however, I realized that – as much as I was happy with my entrepreneurial choice – I was also not at complete peace with the way things had evolved for me at that particular point in time in my career as a lawyer. Around that time, I happened to have a number of casual conversations with other women in positions of similar seniority, all of them lamenting the same problems: the serious delay they were experiencing in moving to the next level, the feeling that everything was meaningless and that it wasn't worth fighting that battle, the enormous difficulty to reconcile rigid working hours with family commitments – most of them having very young children or being in the process of forming a family.

All of a sudden, it hit me like lightning. Was this the infamous glass ceiling that all of us were experiencing? All of us, with a few exceptions, had grown up thinking that the glass ceiling was a myth created by incompetent women and that our technical skills, intelligence and steadfast hard work would have sufficed to breeze through our career.

And yet, there it was, right above our heads, that sheer separation that we kept bumping against and bruising ourselves against without even realizing it.

Once this realization hit me, I felt compelled to do what comes natural to me: I am a learning geek with a passion for knowledge and challenge, and therefore I started researching the issue. I looked for and read any book, article, research and reliable content written on the topic, from the popular *Nice Girls Don't Get the Corner Office*-style books to factual research published by international women's forums and foundations.

I realized how naive I had been in not having educated myself properly before. Especially, I realized how throughout my career I had been lacking some serious, strong female mentors. Yes, I remember some casual conversations with more senior colleagues, but never any serious and engaged mentoring. I remember very few senior women being there, and among them even fewer who would take the time to have a chat with younger colleagues.

For all of these reasons, I decided to initiate a project called the Women Leadership Project. It is a venture dedicated to fostering women's leadership through focused learning, awareness and discussion.

This book is a result of that vision.

I would like to clarify here that this book has very specific focus: it is dedicated to helping women who want to achieve top leadership positions.

We will do it by listening to the opinions and stories of women who have reached top leadership positions, peering into their choices and thoughts. The pathways they have chosen, and their views on what kind of skills, choices, situations and infrastructures are needed for women's ascent to the top.

Although we do not in any way intend to disregard important core issues such as female literacy and education and general gender equality in the workplace[1], we want to focus here on top leadership. We believe that, by advancing women's influence, a new opportunity will be created for a shift in the world's decision-making systems. We believe that, by increasing women's power and influence, the impact on larger issues such as inequality and exploitation of poorer social substrates will be enormous. It has been proved that when women gain more traction in the economy, the overall

---

[1] The World Economic Forum has estimated that closing the remaining employment gender gap in the United States would increase U.S. GDP by up to 9 percent; in BRIC countries, as well as the N-11 nations (Bangladesh, Egypt, Indonesia, Iran, Mexico, Nigeria, Pakistan, the Philippines, South Korea, Turkey, and Vietnam), the Center for Work-Life Policy estimates that utilizing women could push per capita income up by 14 percent by 2020, and 20 percent by 2030. "Study after study," says the White House director of public engagement, Christina Tchen, "shows that increasing education levels and prosperity of women and girls has been able to contribute to social stability and economic progress."

community benefits as a consequence: women are good and conscientious spenders, they spend for themselves, with obvious implications for the growth of the consumer market, but they also tend to spend for their family and invest in community projects much more than men.

Women's power will change the world for the better. We have read studies by McKinsey and by the London Business School suggesting that women in top leadership positions improve business as a whole. But we don't need to read studies to know this. Simply put, women, working in tandem with men at the same level, have a positive transformational impact on business and therefore on society by filling a perspective gap that undoubtedly exists when men sit alone at the tables of power.

# Chapter 1
# The Facts

"Women now drive the world economy", stated the September 2009 Harvard Business Review article *The Female Economy*[2]. Globally, the article went on, they control about USD 20 trillion in annual consumer spending, and that figure could climb as high as USD 28 trillion in the next five years. In aggregate, women represent a growth market bigger than China and India combined.

Fast forward to July 2011. Right after the recession, Newsweek published a new article – *Women Will Rule the World*[3]. According to the article, American women are the breadwinners or co-breadwinners of two-thirds of American households, in the European Union, women filled 75% of the eight million new jobs created since 2000.

Women, it appears, are quickly closing the gender gap at all levels of employment. All levels, that is, except top leadership positions.

The reality is that while women are making their way smoothly and successfully up to middle management, there is a sudden drop in numbers at top management levels. Women work more, and in greater numbers, and they outnumber men in universities and in the first 10

---

[2] The Female Economy, Michael J. Silverstein and Kate Sayre, http://hbr.org/2009/09/the-female-economy/ar/1

[3] http://www.newsweek.com/2010/07/06/women-will-rule-the-world.html

years of top-paying jobs. Then the glass ceiling suddenly appears.

In most organizations, women are not present in the top-most leadership positions. Out of 190 heads of state, only 10% are women. Worldwide, women account for only 13% of parliamentary bodies. And the corporate sector is no different. In Fortune 500 corporations, only 15% of top level executives are women. Closer to home, only 8.9% of directors of Hong Kong's Hang Seng Index companies are women.

The South China Morning Post published an interesting article, on 16 December 2010."Who runs Hong Kong?" Stated the article – "not women". While women make up nearly half of the labour force, men fill 90% of seats on the boards of the largest and most important listed companies.

So what is happening exactly? Why is it that, if women make up more than half of the labour force, even in top-paying positions, there are so few women who make it to the top? Sociologists call this discrepancy the *leaking pipeline.* It is an expression that describes a disturbing phenomenon in which a high number of women quit the workforce when they are in their mid-to-early thirties, just as they are holding mid-management positions and are about to enter the race for top management and leadership positions.

This phenomenon happens worldwide, but what is the specific situation in Asia?

On 6 September 2011, Community Business – a leading non-profit Hong Kong organisation specialising in Corporate Social Responsibility and a leader in diversity and inclusion in Asia – issued the results of a study it conducted on the decreasing presence of women in senior roles. According to Community Business,[4] the phenomenon of the 'leaking pipeline' is very evident in Asia. Across all countries included in the study (China, Malaysia, Hong Kong, Singapore, India and Japan), the representation of women is highest at the junior level and lowest at the senior levels. It decreases by an average of 29.06% from junior to mid-level and accelerates to an average of 48.04% from mid- to senior levels.

With the exception of India, in all these countries the greatest leak (i.e. the largest percentage decrease of women) takes place between mid- and senior level positions. In India the greatest leak takes place at a lower level, between junior and mid-level positions (48.07% decrease).

In Hong Kong, the participating companies do well in overall terms compared to other geographies and have the highest percentage of female representation at mid-level positions across the six geographic regions studied.

Although some of this difference can be explained by the fact that more women are now entering the workforce compared to the previous generation, and therefore some lead time is required for more women to get to top leadership positions, the difference is still too substantial to be ignored.

Shalini Mahtani, who leads Community Business, also personally shared with us during a phone interview that gender bias persists in Hong Kong with the perception, held by most women, that women have to work harder than men to prove themselves or get their voices heard,

---

[4] The 21 companies who tookpart in the benchmark study include: Accenture, AECOM, American Express, Arup, Bank of America Merrill Lynch, Barclays Capital, Cisco, Coca-Cola, DeutscheBank, EMC, Ernst & Young, Goldman Sachs, Herbert Smith, HSBC, Linklaters,Microsoft, Nomura, Schlumberger, Shell, Standard Chartered Bank, UBS.

even though companies insist that that is not the case. The availability of domestic help appears to be a double-edged sword in Hong Kong and may be adding to the expectation for women to work long hours at the expense of time with family – a sacrifice that many are simply not willing to make.

For this reason, in Hong Kong especially, there seems to be an invisible filter, made of an often unbearable pressure that comes with leadership. Men have not yet reached equality with women in the amount of time they spend with and taking care of family (considerably less). It is a natural consequence therefore that women end up pushing themselves to exhaustion, squeezed between the need to be there for their families and the demands of work. When – as a consequence of this struggle - they find themselves sidelined at work or forced to face a slowing career path, they often decide to give up.

# Chapter 2 Women and Leadership

The fact that a glass ceiling is no less prevalent in Hong Kong caught me by surprise? I wondered: how is this possible in Hong Kong, where there are so many educated women?

Philosophically this did not make sense to me. As I often say during my keynote addresses, a new paradigm of leadership has emerged over the last few years, one that is based on awareness, empathy, teamwork and the acceptance of irreconcilable ambiguities. This new paradigm has shattered the old model based on completion of tasks and unilateral directedness.

The older models of leadership were based on warrior skills, the ability to accomplish goals through others. General George S. Patton, US commander during World War II, defined leadership as "the art of getting your subordinates to do the impossible." This was often accomplished through a mix of vision, strength, focus and relentless pursuit of a specific goal, with total and blind conviction, while often disregarding the needs of the members of the team.

The new leader's personality blueprint that has emerged in the last few years not only drives personal achievement and inspires others to follow, but also nurtures and develops a team spirit through attention to principles and each individual's needs, preferences and boundaries. It is developed through the balanced nurturing of physical, intellectual, emotional, and spiritual strength.

At the start of the millennium, Stephen Covey, in his well known reference classic *Principle – Centered Leadership,*[5] discussed the importance of maintaining a balance among personal, family and professional life. He also advocated living by a principle-centered core in order to unleash the creativity, talent, and energy within ourselves and others needed as a leader, and enjoy a more balanced, more rewarding, more effective life.

Consulting companies such as McKinsey[6] have been working on creating models which reflect this new approach, an approach based on nurturing a *power to* accomplish rather than *power over* people. The new leader of the millennium persuades, empowers, collaborates and partners through teamwork, subtle influence, and awareness and respect of others.

The core values that this model embodies – the nurturing, the awareness, the teamwork, the subtle influence – are all traditionally feminine values channeled by women.

And yet, things are not happening, or they are not happening at the speed that we would like. Considering that women's participation in business and politics at the highest levels has been discouraged for millennia, it isn't a surprise that things might take more time than we would hope for. The new generation of working women though is pushing for radical change.

---

[5]*Principle-Centered Leadership,* Stephen Covey, Simon & Schuster, New York, 2003

[6]*How Remarkable Women Lead: The Breakthrough Model for Work and Life*, Joanna Barsch, Crown Business 2009 and https://www.mckinseyquarterly.com/Centered_leadership_How_talented_women_thrive_2193

So what is really going on? For the past few years I have talked to as many women as I could and read as many research reports as I could on this topic, and I have identified three core reasons why women are held back from leadership positions. These same core reasons are the roadblocks that women who make it to the top learn to manage and turn in their favor.

**1. Attitude**

I have often heard women say that they are afraid of the word power. Most women give a negative connotation to the word. As they prefer a leadership style that is inclusive and empathetic rather than commanding, they feel that acknowledging or seeking "power" might corrupt their style. Women may also be afraid to channel a leadership style that is too "masculine" and to seem too ambitious.

In this process, however, they lose some of that directedness that is often needed to compete at very high levels.

So is attitude the problem? Well, partly it is. Although women do not like to speak openly about it, they are actually well-aware that they are ambitious.

Women who are successful, however, learn to own up to their ambition. They learn to be determined, fearless and strong while at the same time not giving up their core values. How do they do this?

**2. Family Commitments**

The struggle for balance between family commitments and work commitments is an issue that doesn't go away. Women are still bearing most of the weight of family duties and, although many men are starting to play a more substantial role by equally partnering with women in the nurturing of children, the fact is that maternity and birth are a woman's gift which places a bigger burden on women.

But does it have to be a curse from a work perspective?

The obvious fact is that during pregnancy and for several months after child-birth women go through an intensive physical and emotional strain that doesn't leave space for much else. It is impossible during that time not to accept that work needs to be slowed down for the sake of one's physical and mental health and that of the baby.

Most women, however, readily accept this and are able to deal with it. The real problem is what happens after the first months of childbirth. This is a very challenging time when women start facing the real difficulty of having to compete in workplaces that often value face-time over results.

As all working moms know, the need to prioritize, be home early to have dinner with your child, and be there when your child needs you requires a tremendous amount of effort, and it is not going to make any of us more competitive in companies where face-time is valued more than actual results.

At the same time, for those of us that work in enlightened companies that value results over quantity of office hours, family commitments would just smoothly fit in with work commitments. This is because (as I can attest having a young toddler) children revolutionize life in a way that makes it impossible to focus on anything else other than work and family, cutting out any other form of distraction. First, they force you to cut down on social commitments and nights out. Second, they necessarily create financial pressure, forcing you to value your work in a different way.

Some companies are reluctant to employ women who are mothers in senior positions because they are afraid that family commitments will take away a woman's focus. My experience (both personal and from talking to other women) is that women who have children are extremely focused, as their life revolves around work and family and they are therefore less distracted by life and removed from the relationship dramas that take time and energy when they are younger.

This does not mean however that it is easy. It takes a strong constitution to deal with the internal guilt that most women feel when they leave home in the morning to go to work.

Women who are successful learn to manage their life by integrating family and work, dealing with the inevitable sense of guilt, not submitting to the pressure of face-time and becoming stronger and more focused. How do they do this?

**3. Issues they face in the workplace and support from their environment**

The final issue is a flip of the coin as it goes back not to women but to their supporting environment. It is very difficult for a woman to move into leadership positions if she doesn't have the right support both at home and at work.

Organizations are now implementing programs and policies for diversity. However there is often a form of hypocrisy where those policies are not implemented in practice. I experienced it when, right after my maternity leave, I asked to be able to work from home one day a week, as was advertised in my organization's intranet as a flexi-time policy available for parents of preschoolers, and I was outright denied the opportunity .

Even though policies are written and good intentions stated, it is still very true that a lot of workplaces simply do not live up to their promises. They don't have solutions in place that help new mothers transition to their new life and they don't have solutions in place for women who are undergoing personal transitions. A lot of companies still value face-time and formal office hours over productivity and results. And let's face it: in any situation where office hours are the parameters for progressing in career, women are not going to be able to compete with men, because for a fact women are rushing out to be home before their children go to bed.

Another issue is the level of travel that senior executives need to be available for, especially in Asia, which becomes prohibitive in child- rearing years.

Women who have been successful have found a way to create around them a support system, at home and at work, that empowers them, allows flexibility and pushes them to be the best they can – often by choosing carefully which organizations to work in. How do they do this and what are those support systems?

I asked myself these questions and I have decided to find the answers by interviewing women who have made it to the top.

In this book, we will hear the voices of women who hold top leadership positions in various industries, and we will hear their stories and their views. The book is divided in two parts: *Part I - Who You Need to Be* focuses on those characteristics that women need to develop and channel. *Part II - What You Need to Ask For* focuses on the support that women need to build in their environment, workplace, and family. All the women we have interviewed embody the characteristics to which they are associated in Part I. However, we thought that the important core message that some others expressed, such as the importance of support systems, environment and opportunities that need to be implemented for women to thrive, required a separate section, hence Part II.

# PART I

# Who We Need To Be

# Chapter 3
# Vision
# Anson Chan

*She's our pioneering mother. To reach her high-profile position as Hong Kong's chief secretary, Anson Chan first had to fight for her basic social and legal rights as a woman -- a far greater battle than the kind most women have had to face after her time. Her modern **VISION** and fierce determination have allowed her to prosper in her career. In the process, she has enabled other women to prosper, too.*

Born in 1940, Anson grew up in a very traditional Chinese family. Girls were brought up very strictly compared to boys. With six brothers and a twin sister, there were a lot of things that were off limits to the two girls.

Luckily, that favoritism wasn't extended to education, on which her family paid great emphasis. This was a critical step in Anson's upbringing because without equal opportunities in education she wouldn't have stood a chance in the workforce.

So the world was a different place for young Anson compared to what it is now, but all over the globe a unified sentiment was simmering in the spirits of hopeful women. After the first feminist movement won the impossible step, at the beginning of the century, in gaining the right to vote across many countries, women worldwide had boarded that rollercoaster ride that is still in motion today. You may call it good fortune, therefore, that the period when young Anson began her career with the Hong Kong government, in the early 1960s, coincided with the second wave of feminism that sought to end all kinds of discrimination, by securing legal and social equality.

At that time, Anson could have easily been a *tai-tai* (as Hongkongers often affectionately call non-working married women with good financial means) if she had so aspired. Her husband, Archibald, an executive at a large oil company, enjoyed all the fringe benefits that could have kept his young wife carefree and entertained. She could have focused all of her energies on raising their two children; it was certainly expected of her. Instead, as a fresh graduate in English literature at Hong Kong University, Anson entered the strictly men-only civil service, after signing up by chance for the competitive entrance exam and passing it despite doubt among her peers.

Over three decades she gracefully navigated her way to the second highest job in the British colony, and made history by becoming not only the first female, but also the first person of Chinese descent to hold the post of chief secretary. Along the way she left a long trail of firsts as first woman assistant financial secretary, first female director of social welfare and first female policy secretary for economic services.

Despite a few hiccups here and there, her accomplishments won her a place in the hearts of many Hong Kong people.

Even today, in her early 70s, while formally retired from the political arena, she keeps her affairs alive from her office in Wanchai. In Hong Kong history books along with her image of perfectly coiffed hair, deep dimples and matching Chanel suits, she will be – if she isn't already – attributed a leading role in handling the transition after the Handover, overseeing the construction of the new airport Chep Lap Kok, stemming corruption, handling foreign diplomacy, ensuring press and personal freedoms and of course, fighting for women's rights.

**Anson's First Battles**

Anson had originally intended to be a social worker but for various reasons she opted to accept the government offer. "It was 1962 and for a cadet a starting salary of $1,200 was a princely sum, despite being 75% of a man's pay, in an equal position," recalls Anson. In fact, the administrative service at that time was almost completely male- dominated with Anson as the second female to join the ranks: a stark contrast to today's scene where women make up at least half of the government workforce.

"When I got married, the requirement in the civil service was to resign and re-apply to be engaged on temporary month-to-month terms," she explains. This meant that other than getting paid less for the same kind of work of male counterparts, the government didn't think married women needed fringe benefits like housing and education allowance for children – these were seen as the husband's responsibilities. In addition, working was supposed to be a pastime for women therefore they shouldn't be taken seriously, they should have considered themselves lucky if they got paid anything at all, an absurd notion that to this day causes Anson to chuckle.

The arrangement was far from ideal but was pervasive. Anson and her female colleagues, who had in the meantime increased in numbers, stalled for a few years hoping that the main staff union would do something about the gender discrimination. They waited, and waited, but nothing happened. Finally, breathing that air of change that was coming with the second wave of feminists and realizing that they had to take matters into their own hands, Anson and a group of 12 women formed a trade union to fight for equality of pay and fringe benefits which they eventually secured fully in 1982, over a decade later.

While this battle was taking place, Anson delved into promoting women's education, a critical step in attaining gender equality. In the 1970s, she was involved in a very significant expansion of educational opportunities and in setting up the equal opportunities commission to enact legislation that outlawed sexual discrimination.

**Becoming a Leader**

"The woman's role was very much stereotyped in those days and there was a very clear design of what they should be doing or not doing, particularly among very traditional Chinese families," explains Anson. Her role was meant to be in the home with the family and it was considered a huge compliment if people said to you: "You are equally good at home in the kitchen and presentable in the living room."

While most women were perfectly happy being somebody's wife and bringing up children, Anson enjoyed working and was often questioned by male friends and colleagues about her ambition. "I don't think I was particularly ambitious," dismisses Anson. "I was very fortunate in that the administrative service most of my bosses, all of whom were men, were all extremely good people. Good not only for having a high sense of integrity, but also as far as intellectual abilities and intellectual honesty."

According to Anson, those bosses all showed concern for their junior staff – male or female – and genuinely sought to impart their knowledge and teach their staff how to best argue one's case or write a succinct paper that would be considered by the Executive Council. As such, the young Anson was regularly monitored and supported.

Anson credits this support and mentoring in her early working years as one of the building blocks that enabled her to gain self-confidence. She was lucky to have found good mentors in her bosses.

Determination also played a key role in Anson's career. She says, "It applies to both men and women that if you want to succeed in anything you have to have the determination and perseverance – you can't expect to get something for nothing." Anson adds, "You have to put your back to it, keep your eyes wide open and you need to tell yourself, I'm learning on the job which is usually how your bosses teach you."

A strong ethical foundation is another key to leadership, she says. "To be a good leader you need to lead by example. Leadership must be ethical. You can't have leadership where there is no sense of values, where people have no sense of integrity." Acknowledging the lasting impression that her bosses made on her as well as the influence of her upbringing, Anson asserts, "Today increasingly among executives anything goes, so long as you're not found out. There is also the attitude in which the end justifies the means. I don't subscribe to either."

**Managing Yourself**

As Anson climbed the career ladder, her job got significantly more demanding. At the same time, pressures at home were mounting with a husband and two children to look after. If there are few role models today of women who successfully integrate family and work, there were even fewer examples during that time. Anson had to rely on her own instincts and on the wisdom that had been passed down from the women in her family.

First of all, she says, to manage a career and a family is not always easy and there are a few things you have to accept.

"You cannot expect the best of all worlds, not when you are juggling three different hats. Mine were: a reasonable career, I'm somebody's wife and somebody's mother. So you constantly have to juggle these three worlds and you have to accept that all three worlds won't be perfect at all times."

At different stages of your career, simultaneous with your children's development, your priorities change, Anson observes. For example when her children were very young, sometimes Anson had to tell them that she couldn't take them to school that day. Fortunately her husband's mother stayed with them and helped out with the kids.

Even so, Anson was a hands-on figure in the education of her children, who never had tutors throughout primary school. She sat with them on most days, when she could, and went through their homework. But by the time they got to secondary school, she expected her children to be responsible and independent. She told them she wouldn't look over their shoulders all the time because they had to learn to study on their own, but she would look at their schoolwork from time to time and if she found that they hadn't been applying themselves, they'd be suitably punished.

"So I think you need to have that sense of proportion and you have to accept that at the best of times you are not going to have the best of all worlds," says Anson. "As a consequence you have to be forgiving of yourself.

I know that sometimes women are prevented from moving up the ladder because they have this guilty feeling that they're not spending enough time with their children or their husbands think that they are too career-minded. Well, you have to be forgiving of yourself, tell yourself, 'If my choice is to have a career, get married and have children, well, then sometimes, something will have to give'."

Whether you have children and/or a husband, it's important to learn how to say, "No," Anson says. Many women don't know how to do that and as a result are overwhelmed by work responsibilities and can't carve out enough personal time.

When Anson first became chief secretary, a high-profile and extremely demanding job, she used to work on average 12 hours a day. She'd get to the office around 7.30am and very often had to entertain or be entertained until past midnight.

One of her initial adjustments in the new position was to ask her staff, if possible, to keep Tuesdays free so she could spend some time with her mother. She also tried to get most weekends free to spend more time with her family but that didn't mean that she got every one of those days free. At least, she says, by getting that message across, reasonable people would try to work around her schedule because they'd realize it wasn't that unreasonable. On her side instead, she had to accept that sometimes it was unavoidable to have activities over the weekend, as many NGOs, staffed by volunteers, have time only then.

Many women leave the workforce not only because they are consumed by guilt, but because they are stuck in their own disparaging image of their own abilities and potential. Some women think they are only good enough to reach a certain level. "I used to feel the same way when I joined the government," says Anson. "I'd say to myself: 'I'll be very happy if I become the deputy head of a department because then I still have time for my family', but as I got more experienced, I got more exposure, I learnt more and my expectations rose until I began to say to myself: 'Ah maybe, after all…it's not so difficult to move one rung up the ladder!'"

Looking back at her career she says she probably wouldn't have been picked to be the chief secretary before the handover if she hadn't had the right kind of work experience. Her preparation for the post came from her seven years as secretary for economic services characterized by its heavy portfolio dealing with major issues such as building an international airport, expanding the port, deregulating the telecommunications industry, and so on.

"If I had not acquired the experience and done that job I don't think Chris Patten would have thought that I really had the experience for the chief secretary's job. I wouldn't call it luck, but being in the right place at the right time."

**40% Rule?**

Some European countries have implemented a "40% rule" that stipulates at a minimum this percentage of women on the board and in the upper echelons of companies. With her extensive experience in government and in securing women's rights, Anson's opinion on a possible regulation in Hong Kong remains lukewarm.

"I'm of two minds about this," she says. "I'm not sure whether it's the best way forward, but that said, I accept that if in an organization as a result of years of stereotyping and bias, women have never been given the opportunity, you probably do need – even if for a limited period – some form of affirmative action. But I think the best is still to effect a fundamental change in the way people look at the female workforce in their subconscious thinking."

While it would be better to let people go through career obstacles on their own, sometimes, as Anson points out, it is necessary to enforce changes such as when she de-regularized the telecommunications market. That opened up the playing field to new and worthy competitors that would have otherwise been cordoned off. As a result the industry as a whole became stronger. The reality is that most people are wavering on this issue.

Anson thinks it is encouraging that many corporations are accepting that you need to provide some support services if you are going to allow women to move up the career stream. First you have to accept that they get married and have children. Then you should be conscious that they are clearly worried about their children, as men should be. So sometimes, as an employer you may have to be more tolerant on working hours, you need to provide some support services, and these days with information technology, maybe you can even introduce flexi-time and allow people to work at home.

"The other thing is there has to be a culture – the same as ethics – from the very top all the way to the lower ranks that recognizes that women are a valuable human resource," says Anson. "Let's face it. At the end of the day, despite modern technology and all the help you get with machines, for any organization the most precious capital is human capital. Therefore it's worth a company investing in ensuring that you maximize on this human capital."

She adds that today in a lot of professions there seem to be more and more women joining the ranks, even in financial services. While this is certainly true, the other face of the coin shows that when women enter traditionally male-dominated professions there comes a point in their career when they decide to leave – usually in mid-management positions, in their mid-thirties – often after giving birth to their first or second child.

**Being a Woman Who is the Best Man for the Job**

As chief secretary, Anson was often asked what it felt like to be the principal woman and she used to say: "I happen to be the best man for the job." The word "man", she explains, is used in a totally gender-neutral way and that is the way you want to be considered. She says that one doesn't want to be the token woman in any board -- you want to be taken seriously and recognized for your own abilities, purely on merit.

Some women seem to think, however, that equality of the sexes is about being as macho as males. Anson couldn't disagree more, saying that even though she's quite happy to be more than equal, she definitely enjoys having a gentleman open her door. But some women, when they aspire to a particular job somehow learn the worst attributes of men and emulate conduct that is counter-productive to effective communication and harmonious interpersonal relationships.

"Women should acknowledge first of all that they are women!" emphasizes Anson, adding that in the average woman there are certain qualities that are more pronounced than in the male: such as empathy, compassion, maybe not so much insistence on form rather than substance. These are all qualities that she says women should take some pride in.

One of the possible reasons women tend to assume male traits is that up to now there haven't been enough female role models in leadership positions. It's important for leaders to be comfortable in their own skin, says Anson. While men seem to think it's not masculine to cry or to show emotions, Anson believes everybody would feel better by sometimes letting go of their emotions, instead of keeping everything bottled up.

She recalls one instance when she was told she was too emotional. Baffled, she replied: "Define what you mean by emotional? If you mean I feel passionately about certain things, yes, I do. I think it's important to have real passion for what you are doing. It's not a 9-to-5 job, so if you don't have the passion you don't throw yourself into it and then you do a passable, mediocre job."

**Role Models**

Anson's mother, Fang Zhaoling, was her greatest inspiration. So was her paternal grandmother, who was illiterate and grew up in the days when it was still traditional for women to have bound feet. Only later did her grandmother realize that binding, which resulted in her feet being deformed, was not a good thing. But despite her grandmother's illiteracy and misfortune, she had an extremely strong character and ruled the family with an iron hand – a trait that Anson positively inherited.

Her mother was widowed in her mid-30s with eight children: the oldest being only 11 (Anson and her twin sister were 10) and the youngest brother was 3. In her generation she wasn't expected to remarry and she brought the kids up with her grandmother, aunts and uncle chipping in – luckily they were a very close-knit family. What's more is that Ms. Fang not only managed to bring up eight children; she carved out an extremely successful career for herself as a very talented and resourceful painter.

The walls of Anson's office are adorned by a set of paintings from her late mother. She proudly illustrates the artist's distinctive style that evolved over 40 years, ultimately resulting in a blend of sophisticated yet simple brushstrokes – a rare combination to attain. When we find out she had studied with Zhang Daqian and Zhao

Shao'ang, two of the foremost masters in modern Chinese art, we are even more impressed by her unique style.

"My mother was good at everything," says Anson. "She used to make all our clothes. She was a good cook. She travelled widely and had a great generosity of spirit. Almost nothing lowered her, although she went through a tough time financially, when she was in London with three of my brothers, but she could never kept down for too long."

Ms. Fang painted until her early 90s and taught Anson how to persevere, how to ignore things that really shouldn't matter; she was a very forgiving person herself. Anson stresses that the most important thing for any leader is to know who you are and what you want to be because if you don't know then you will always tend to sit on the fence and bend with the wind.

"To have integrity means to have the courage of your convictions even when everybody else tells you, 'You are wrong.' In fact, integrity is most important when everyone around you is going this way and your conscience tells you, 'No, you should be going the other way.' When you don't have the comfort of peer influence, you have to stick your neck out – that takes a very strong conviction," she says.

**Hard Times**

While Anson never doubted she was on the right career path, there were moments when things were going really badly. "I had the press on my back, I had a very difficult boss, but you learn to take that in your stride." She only really had one career, entirely in the public service but it helped to keep the job fresh as she usually got a new posting every two or three years until becoming secretary of economic services and chief secretary, positions which each lasted 7 years.

The administrative work stayed the same but the people and policies involved were totally different from one post to the other. This meant there was never a dull moment, as she always learned something new and got satisfaction from the work that she was doing. For example, Anson says, if you were posted to the government secretariat, essentially the nerve center of the Hong Kong government, you would have less contact with grassroots people. You would tend to sit behind your desk and look at issues, have meetings, and work out policies. In contrast, when posted to a department like social welfare or commerce and industry, not only would you be involved in policy-making but the much stronger human aspect of those positions meant you would see the results of training younger colleagues and helping them to develop.

"You have to be there to support junior staff and you learn where the buck stops," she explains. "It stops with you as the director. When something goes wrong, even if you may have had nothing to do with it, as the director you take the blame, in the same way you take the credit for what's going right. By doing this, your staff respects you so much more because they know you're there for them even when things go wrong."

In the same vein, Anson believes that when something goes wrong, you don't bully your staff in public. Instead, you take corrective action in private, and, publicly, the leader should take the blame. "You can't say, 'I had nothing to do with this, it was my junior officer.' It's not the way for a leader to behave," she says.

## Changing Values and Marriage

Anson witnessed some of the most exciting times in the path to women's empowerment. There have been great shifts in the way women are viewed by society, and in the expectations family impose upon them. Marriage, as a consequence has evolved into a more lax institution, with divorce rates soaring all over the globe.

Anson believes this phenomenon is attributable to modern women, many of whom are now well-educated, and regard themselves every bit as good, if not better than men. With flourishing careers, they don't have to depend on men, they don't have to put up with things they don't like in the marriage; in general there is less tolerance to put up with things that don't always go their way.

"In my days there was a much greater level of tolerance," says Anson, adding that it wasn't a bad quality, especially when linked to relationships. "Youngsters today seem to regard marriage as a sort of battleground," says Anson. "I tell young people when they ask me to talk about marriage: 'First, marriage is not a battle, you don't have to win each and every fight. Sometimes it is better if you keep your mouth shut, then you don't say things that upset the other person because people seem to forget that what you say, you may apologize for later but it cannot be erased." We echo that sentiment and add that tolerance and respect for each other are qualities that should extend to every aspect of one's life, and by cultivating them in one's home they can then more easily be adopted in other circumstances.

In closing, Anson would like to encourage young ambitious women to recognize that their future is in their hands. "You should make the most of the opportunities that come your way," she says. "The sky is the limit, but whatever choices you make, you have to live with those choices and their consequences."

# Chapter 4
# Determination
# Deborah Kan

*She went from being told that she didn't stand a chance in the industry to becoming an international TV journalist. With unrelenting* ***DETERMINATION*** *Deborah Kan got into financial news without ever having worked in finance before. She chooses to work because she loves her job, and she feels this makes her a better mother.*

Deborah kicks off our interview by telling us about a recent trip to North Korea with the New York Philharmonic. As she describes the peculiar facets of the infamously secretive nation, we hold our breath, waiting to hear about the moment when she will stray off from the official tour group, hoping to discover some of the truths that are carefully concealed to outsiders. Finally the moment comes. While her minder is distracted she runs out of the hotel for a solitary jog in the quiet yet populous streets of Pyongyang. The story goes on to unravel big surprises, but that's a story that's hers to tell. What is obvious from the onset though, is that this woman has a strong, independent personality.

**"And I am telling you, you don't have it"**

When Deborah Kan landed her first two journalism gigs she was on a roll. As an English degree graduate with experience working for the campus radio station, her only entry point into the notoriously zipped up TV journalism world was to get herself an internship, which she secured. With that under her belt, she found a job as a news messenger at San Francisco's local TV station and despite the lack of glamour she was thrilled to have broken into the industry.

Things sailed smoothly thereafter. Deborah thought her career was on a really good track. Between filling up the gas tanks of huge satellite vans and driving tapes from bureau to bureau, she dreamed about what her next step would be. With her mixed American/Chinese good looks and energetic charisma, becoming a TV reporter wasn't that unthinkable. So she put together a resume tape and sent it to a job posting in a picturesque town on the California coast, south of San Francisco.

Eager to secure an encounter, she followed up with a phone call to the news director. "I'm right for this job and want to come down and see you," Deborah recalls saying. She exuded so much confidence that he agreed in a heartbeat and she thought, "Yes! I got the interview. I'm on my way. This feels right."

Without stopping once, Deborah drove to California and five hours later was sitting in the TV station's bland conference room decorated only with a California poster on the wall. After watching her tape for about seven minutes, the news director, pushed eject, handed her back the tape and told Deborah, "There are people who have it in this business and those who don't and I'm telling you, you don't have it so get out of the business before you waste any more time."

## Turning Failures into Success

Devastated, she got back into her car. She cried her eyes out as she drove back home. But about halfway, while driving on the highway, something great happened: she got angry, really angry. She was so infuriated that anyone could belittle her, that the news director's rejection became her source of empowerment, popping up in her mind as a reminder every time she felt insecure. That moment was so powerful, she was so determined to prove him wrong, that to this day, he still comes back in her mind to give her a shove when she needs it.

In retrospect, as traumatic as it may have been, that conference room encounter was a good thing to happen to a 21 year old. It started a mechanism of self-defense at an age that for Deborah (and for many others too) was about being insecure about her abilities and throwing herself out there always questioning right from wrong. That attitude later transformed into focus on getting established and building a reputation in her 30s. And as soon as she turned 40, Deborah hit a new stage of poise and confidence where things that seemed vital before didn't matter anymore.

"If I fail now it's okay," she says with a smile. "I feel like it's a whole different attitude, through maturity you get more confidence. If I only had the confidence in my 20s that I have now…" We sigh and laugh it out, thinking back at our own conflicted pasts. "In your 20s you're cockier because you haven't failed enough. Somebody said to me that his biggest failures were his biggest successes, and I believe that's very true because you need to know what it's like to fail in order to succeed at certain things."

## Coming to Hong Kong

After the rejection, she returned to her duties of news messenger and continued to apply for jobs in small markets in the US. Around that time, she visited her grandmother in Hong Kong and her father suggested she try applying to a TV station here. Hong Kong at that point wasn't on her radar since she had various reasons keeping her tied to San Francisco; nonetheless she was curious of the outcome. So, one morning while visiting Hong Kong she took a tour of TVB, dropped off her tape and returned to the US without thinking twice about it.

Four months later when she received a letter from TVB, she had nearly forgotten that she had applied. There was an opening for a reporter and she was offered the job. Torn by the unexpected news, she thought hard for about 30 seconds but soon realized: how could she pass on such an opportunity when her alternatives were small local stations in the US?

Talking live on TV is a talent that takes time and practice to master; it's not quite as natural as it looks. The usual rite of passage for a young reporter is to cover the weather and quite often that first time isn't easily forgotten. Deborah was no exception. "I remember feeling like I could never do a live shot; it was so scary, talking to the camera <u>live</u>." Her first assignment was to cover a typhoon and back in the day the reporter was pretty much tied to a post and put in the windiest wave-whipping place possible.

As she struggled to keep it together, worrying about being unable to answer unexpected questions from the anchor, the light went on in the camera. She adjusted her ear piece and as she started speaking another voice seemed to be speaking to her, and it wasn't the anchor's. She paused. Panic. She started speaking and again she heard that voice, she stopped. No one had told her that she could experience a delay in her voice that day and she was so nervous that she didn't immediately realize it was her own. She figured it out pretty quickly but the sensation was unsettling. She kept thinking: "I can't do this, I can't do this…what was I saying?" That's when the news director appeared to her for the first time since that day on the highway. Determined not to make a fool of herself, she ploughed through and the rest is history.

**Financial News and Sexing It Up**

20 years, a husband and three kids later, she accepted a job as the leading business news presenter at Thomson Reuters. The typhoon experience was only one of many challenges Deborah has had to overcome. The latest is becoming a financial reporter.

"When I first got started it was intimidating because I had never worked in finance before and felt like I didn't really get it" she confesses. Yet with her usual determination she dove into the subject and after two years of what felt to her like business school, Deborah re-emerged more confident than ever.

Deborah tells us that – even in a sector so specific and professional as finance – the TV business is trying to determine what kind of content the audience wants. If you look at mainstream TV, whether it is finance news or not, the message is quite obvious: the audience wants to see attractive women sexing it up.

Now, sure this is an old argument, but in this context, we ask Deborah how much femininity she is willing to put on display to get better results. These days most news channels are sexed up and even the most reputed financial programs have women walk around the newsroom then casually sit on a desk - and when they are wearing a skirt you can't help but notice, 'Oh there's her leg.' If men rule the financial world, it's no surprise women financial reporters are in demand.

"We had this discussion in the newsroom and I made it clear that I find that shot completely inappropriate," says Deborah bluntly. "It just doesn't look professional. It's a cheap decoy to get people interested. But the problem is that those programs get the numbers and even if you're against it, it's still what it is and you can't really counter that because it's a business in the end. It's going to keep happening. I think as an individual you can decide whether or not you're comfortable with it and say you aren't going to do that."

But there's a flip side to it too. While Deborah says she has never experienced discrimination per se, she has been in meetings where people tell her she should interview a certain person because he is a pervert. "I don't tend to take things like this extremely seriously and at first you go 'Oh yeah, whatever,' but then afterwards I think about it and wonder what was that the right thing to say? What about my brain? I'm a good interviewer and that's why I should do the interview, not because I'm a woman."

Other than these issues that are up to each woman to decide how to handle, the glass ceiling seems to be less impenetrable for women in the media. An equal distribution of men and women make up the editorial and management side. Yet this doesn't rule out difficulties in flexibility in the workplace.

**Setting Realistic Expectations**

As a working mother – and with a husband also working full-time – Deborah still feels like the primary caretaker of the family. "You can argue and debate whether that's right or wrong but I think that's the reality in most women's lives," she says. "I always say that I aspire to have a stay-at-home dad as a husband and put the pressure on them, you know… but I really believe that as long as society is set up that way and the woman provides the primary care for the children then it's going to come down to striking a balance. It's an issue that a lot of women face."

So if a company wants to keep women in the workforce there has to be some sort of give and take. “That’s why a lot of women turn away from finance. It’s not the only reason but I look at my husband’s schedule. He’s on a plane all the time, he works long hours and as a woman I don’t want that. It’s not worth it to me.”

In her current job she was able to negotiate better hours for herself so she could go in earlier and could try and leave at about 4.30pm every day. Even if it doesn’t work out every single day it’s better than getting home at 8pm. When she was working at STAR TV and handling the late news it was very hard for her. She had her third child and wasn’t getting home till 8.45pm. “It’s funny because now that I’m out of that routine, I think, ‘How did I do that?’ and ‘Why did I do that?’ It was so silly,” she says. “It’s easy to get caught in the situation and feel like this is what you have to do, it’s your job. But you really do have alternatives.

“Once I stepped out I realized I didn’t want that anymore. I decided that for the next job I wanted to get home at a decent hour and I wasn’t going to compete with people who don’t have to rush home or attend two-hour school meetings. It’s part of my reality and I’m not going to make excuses for it.”

Hearing Deborah talk so openly about her choice, and the fact that some jobs are more compatible with home duties while others – realistically – are not, really gives us a sense of relief and also of opportunities. There are different choices out there that can be made without compromising one’s professional achievements and ambitions. Searching for a job that allows you to grow, while being compatible with home commitments – rather than fighting a losing battle every day – is not only practical but also extremely smart.

The best thing to have is realistic expectations, says Deborah. "If you want something bad enough, you can have it, you will get it, but I think the key is to set your expectations from the very beginning." Even if you found a great job and thought you really want to do it but it's going command 12-to-14 hour days, she asks, are you really going to be happy? "The secret is to set the expectations upfront and if the place of employment doesn't want that, then it's not the right match."

With her husband as the main breadwinner of the family, Deborah feels privileged to have the choice of working or not. This affects the way you look at things and your motivation. "If I get into a situation in which I decide I don't like my job anymore, I can walk away from it," she concedes. "But I'm working because I love what I do."

And she's lucky to have found a supportive husband. She took four and half years off work while her children were young, and she never felt like she was unhappy. Ironically her husband pushed her to go back to work because he could feel she was a happier person working than not. "I guess it's just my personality," Deborah recalls. "He said that I need something of my own that I can independently throw my energy into that's separate from my kids and my family. And I think I'm a better mom for that, I can appreciate my kids more. It really depends what kind of person you are. There are some wonderful women who are energized through staying at home and being with their children and that's great."

Yet she feels she isn't the perfect mother. She is always forgetting something and she is notorious for accepting birthday party invitations and then her kid won't show up because she forgot about it. "I wonder what other moms think of me," she admits. But that's the way it goes, nobody ever said it was easy. "Sometimes I'm great, sometimes I'm terrible," she adds.

Luckily at work there is an incredible environment where there are several working moms constantly running in and out of the office. That setting is conducive to allowing women to have a full-time career.

"If I didn't have that [career], the pressure would build up even more," says Deborah. "If I worked in an environment where people didn't have families, male or female, I don't think they could really understand what my needs would be, because I wouldn't have before having kids. So you do the best you possibly can but it's never easy."

It's not just the structure of the company that makes a difference; it's also the people. Knowing that you can run out for a couple of hours and no one is going to bat an eyelash makes life much easier. A friend of Deborah's recently left her job in finance because some days she had to rush for a school meeting and then she'd rush back to work feeling guilty. That's a terrible feeling to have because what she's doing is for her kid is indeed important.

We agree with Deborah that working with a supportive team who has similar views on how work and life need to be balanced and integrated is the best solution. As our interview nears its end, we ask her what kind of solutions companies could put in place to foster women's careers and provide even more flexibility. Deborah is strongly in favor of job sharing, a solution practiced with success in some US companies where two people share the same role and work as a team to cover one position. In a world where 24/7 connectivity is a requirement, part-time work can be detrimental to career progression, says Deborah, but job sharing is not – the work is covered seamlessly and the two partners share the role progress together. It is real cooperation – and an interesting possibility.

# Chapter 5
# Purpose
# Christine Loh

*She went from being a commodities trader to a politician, and today Christine Loh channels her passion through Civic Exchange, a think tank that works for the public interest. With admirable **PURPOSE** she inspires others to become concerned citizens and better human beings. She is passionate about everything and has won multiple awards that attest to her outstanding efforts.*

Inside the Civic Exchange office, silence reigns, although the room is brimming with people. Judging by the focused facial expressions, most of the noise is going on inside their heads. Sitting behind computers or sketching on notepads, the busy bees are looking for solutions, securing funding and researching ways to improve the lives of the Hong Kong community. A few moments later we meet their leader, Christine Loh, and are seated around a table in the open space.

"They are all very focused in this kind of work," she says softly to explain the quiet. Their latest project is to create an index that measures a city's well-being – a first of its kind in Asia – which in turn would give them clarity on what they need to do to improve the items on the index that are not going well. Civic Exchange is active in social, economic and environmental spheres with all three fields intertwining with one other. Original ideas that are multi-disciplinary and cross cultural excite the Civic Exchange staff the most. "I see many issues as linked, probably as a result of my political experience," says Christine who in the past decade has been one of Hong Kong's most vocal watchdogs in protecting the environment and promoting greater democracy.

It's fitting, then, that all employees would share Christine's same passion and righteousness. "I'm interested in solutions," says the woman who interestingly pulled out from the political arena to do just that. She was a legislator for several years and in 2000 gave up running for re-election – that she was expected to win –to start the think tank with her chief legislative aide, Lisa Hopkinson.

Christine had been quietly thinking of alternatives for herself in case she didn't win the election. She knew she wasn't interested in returning to the commercial sector and she wanted to create change in different areas of the city's welfare. That's when she realized that she was getting more excited about the idea of operating in the non-profit sector than being in the Legislative Council.

**Evolving, Changing**

Because the passage of time changes perspectives, Christine says that at different times she has looked at herself differently. Now, at 55, she says she's tasted enough bitterness to know a few things – a stark contrast to her 20s, when she says she knew nothing (who does at that age?). She started out in a big company as a commodities trader and at that point was just trying to learn and figure out what was going on. After that came her public life as a politician. At present, she says she is in a more reflective mode. "Today, I focus on using what

I know, what resources I have to enable others to act because now I know I can only do so much," Christine says.

It is a winning combination that Christine has adopted and a significant trait of good managers: she does more by teaming up and facilitating others. Compared to a 25-year-old she has more focus, more experience, a longer rolodex and has a certain perspective. But what younger people have – that she no longer has, and this is fundamental – is the ability to really put their shoulder to the wheel.

"Until my mid-thirties, I didn't know what the word 'tired' meant," explains Christine. "I was tremendously fit and I used to go running for two hours before going to work. I was unencumbered. I didn't have a worry in the world: no sick parents, no real personal problems and no responsibilities. I was just responsible for myself."

But it was during her political tenure that she developed the visionary mission and strong sense of purpose she possesses today. When she was younger, most goals had no bigger dimension than herself and her immediate family.

"Once you get into public life you realize that things you can do could change things for the whole community," she says. "This is like a really big thought which is why I'm very interested in politics." It's true, politics can be scary and people often don't trust politicians, but we can't disregard that the work they do is truly important. It has a potential to change the lives of many others.

"That's when I felt I had a calling. Every time I went to work as a politician I felt I could do something and that is still what is propelling me forward." As a public policy think tank, the public interest is at the core of Civic Exchange's work. And the enabling of others goes to the extent that they will raise money for other NGOs and other individuals too because that's part of their mission. Not many other organizations could say the same.

Looking back, Christine feels like her previous experiences were building up for this mission. "I believe in fate and destiny and many times over the years I've asked myself, 'What is the purpose of my life?'" Indeed, she has had a privileged life. She has not been through great suffering nor had any great insight. But, she is mindful that she "got dropped in places that gave me a certain experience and a heightened awareness of my environment."

**Killer Skills**

She first thought she was going to be a lawyer but became a commodities trader instead. Learning how international business was done, she rose very quickly in the company but modestly points out that it wasn't that difficult since there weren't many people in her field in those days. That's why she says it's about being in the right place at the right time. In other words, that is destiny but the rest depends on what you make of it.

She did reasonably well, she says, not because she was brilliant but because she kept at it. She says that early on she was conscious about not being the cleverest person around (though we doubt that). On the other hand she noticed she had an assemblage of skills that made people quite comfortable with her. And she realized those skills were really important because many other people who were smarter didn't get so far.

"I have a huge capacity to listen. So I can always understand what the other person is saying and I can paraphrase," Christine says. "This is like a killer app, applicable in any business." For example, her boss would send her to a two-hour meeting and in 30 seconds she could tell him what the most important thing was. "I didn't actually realize I had these skills and I couldn't even articulate what they were until I was in my late 20s, when I realized that people were really impressed by my ease in relating an actual factual summary."

That wasn't all. To complement her oral skills, she could also write great summaries. "So I'm not the person with the original thought, I'm the person that can put it down so everyone can say, 'Ah, so that's what happened,' and in turn it enables them to make decisions." This is how she made her name when she was young.

It's interesting how such basic skills can be so vital. Christine over the years has worked with many well-informed people who are unable to communicate their knowledge. So basically this is what they do at Civic Exchange: they try to understand and reprocess information in a way that ordinary people can understand, too. "Ours is seldom action," she explains. "For example, you want to clean up the environment. I can't do it myself. It's always some industry or sector of the government or somebody else who has to act. Our role is to take some complex stuff, put it in some context so that decision makers can grasp the issue and hopefully take some action. So there's the 200-page version of the report, there's the 10-page summary, and there's the two page leaflet, and now I guess you have to be able to do the Twitter line, too."

**Early Mentor**

Just as most women interviewed for this book, Christine found a mentor at the beginning of her career, an Australian gentleman who was her immediate supervisor and to this day remains a friend. He would give her some work and then leave the office. "What I didn't know at the time was that he obviously had some confidence in me, otherwise he wouldn't disappear. But I always knew that if I had a problem I could always contact him and ask him." She recalls this as being extremely useful for a number of reasons. First, he gave her the chance; second, he was very secure in himself and didn't feel threatened by her; and third, as a younger person who knew relatively little, she realized that she was lucky she could learn fast. Obviously her confident personality also helped her along the way in gaining the trust of her superiors.

Christine never saw being a woman as a disadvantage; in fact it was quite the contrary. Commodity trading was a vastly male-dominated business so around 6pm all the male traders would end up in the most senior trader's room drinking whiskey. This is how the old boys' club bonded, with the ones attending the gathering often being particularly close to the boss. Of course Christine, being a girl, never went nor was expected to go. This didn't mean that they were unkind to her. She was the youngest there by a long stretch and did her work without ever failing on the performance.

Again, when it came to socializing with customers she'd have a lunch occasionally but wasn't obliged to entertain them in the evenings, so she just stuck to business. She became very well known among her clients because there weren't many women working in the business at that time and she was pleasant to deal with. Working for one of the biggest companies, she understood that some of the Chinese companies would always give them a good slice of the business because they could be assured of performance. Eventually, she became regional managing director.

### Diversity and Managing Talent

Christine feels that there are still relatively few companies that think about how to bring the best out of their workers, despite the vast amount of literature on how to nurture talent, and within that, how to have more women in the workforce. Christine acknowledges there is a new positive focus on diversity in companies, however how much is actually done in practice is very much dependent on their leader. "The focus on diversity can go away from one CEO to another. I'm not yet sure if we can say that this way of thinking is well-embedded in our society when people look at diversity."

Whether or not we talk about women, the real issue here is that commercial companies find it difficult to provide a lot of flexibility for their workers. Christine likens the current situation to a kind of industrial work style, where division of labor is supreme. "At the most basic end it's people coming in and punching a card and the more that you make this efficient the better is the outcome from the company's point of view, so work has to be standardized and they all do this one thing." But today we are looking at a more knowledge-based society that requires a completely different mindset, so can we really look at individual talent and make him or her fit with another 500 people?

"I'm not sure there are many companies looking at it this way," says Christine. "They will say they have a business [to run] and have to get their business done." As a result many companies in our so-called information/knowledge world may still be operating like an industrial enterprise.

Christine strongly feels that the focus should be on talent and how to deal with it in a practical, meaningful way. And when dealing with talented women this means fully internalizing the fact that at a certain age they are going to be mothers.

So how are companies going to provide flexibility without undermining their business objectives?

"The production mindset of human resource management is about: the more standard I can make it, the better: same contracts, same terms…so I think this is the crux of the issue. How can we manage an organization with some degree of standardization that allows the individual to make a lot of choices?" says Christine, hitting upon a chronic difficulty for most companies.

Companies shouldn't be afraid of diversity and flexibility. Sure, needing 20 different contracts as opposed to only one may sound like a great headache, and most companies would immediately say it's too complicated. "So one way to start out would be to have a fair but more diverse management system, but it does take time," says Christine. It also requires that you find out from a majority of individuals in the company what would be considered fair. You can see it as building a new ethos and accompanying that ethos with an operating system: an upgraded management system that would allow more diversity and therefore keep more talent within the company. This would also allow for different types of contractual arrangements.

A change of this caliber needs strong support from the top leadership of the company, however it would not only help retain senior talented women but also make the company a valuable place to work in for the younger generation, which grew up in an age of maximum flexibility and expects to find the same at work.

"The world is different and we expect different kind of work from the young. So the workplace is going to have to accommodate this [mentality]" says Christine.

There is a whole new generation of people who share women's need for flexibility and the way into the future is for companies to learn to deal with this complexity.

Christine suggests looking at one more place to find some answers. Big companies and consulting companies don't generally look at small companies to find solutions for themselves. "I suspect there are good business models around: smaller companies can innovate." They have often been overlooked because it's unlikely that a Harvard Business School is going to come study their model, and when they are bought, the focus is on the brand or product, not the business model.

Finally, putting women in executive roles may help, but it does not necessarily solve the problem either. Perhaps, she suggests, the easiest thing to do is just to be a decent human being because sometimes it is really hard to change the system. Even as a CEO you cannot control what the company does because you still have the board, the chairman and decades of practices to crack. You can't change it all overnight. "But there is one thing you can do immediately and at any time, and that is to be a decent person" says Christine. You may then ask yourself, how do you choose to influence a long-term process while you are there?

# Chapter 6
# Fearlessness
# Marie-Amélie Hoffman

*When Tiger Woods says: "Giving up is not an option" in a well known commercial, Marie-Amélie Hoffman gets the goose bumps. She's had her fair share of challenges, including running her own trading business in Mexico. She has always tackled them with relentless **FEARLESSNESS.** Today she sits at the pinnacle of one of the most powerful companies in the luxury industry.*

"I've always felt like life is exciting but things have been tough," says Marie-Amélie. She describes herself as always searching for different things to rattle her comfort zone, so she is partly responsible for her moments of quandary, as well as her moments of pride. Her stamina apparently comes from a very demanding father who made her feel like nothing was ever good enough, instilling in her a desire to always reach higher.

When she first moved to Hong Kong in 2009 to take up her current role as the GM of LVMH Watches and Jewelry, she even got a gastric ulcer. In the space of a few months, the pressures of a new job, new city, new everything proved difficult to adapt to but the biggest blow came when the financial crisis hit that same year.

Now that the eye of the storm has passed and things have settled, Marie-Amélie would say the turbulent beginning was all worth it. She's definitely not the kind that enjoys lamenting.

That's something she doesn't share with the many women who get stuck in unfulfilling situations. She warns them that to make real changes in their lives they first have to change the way they see things. "Women think that just by being good, good will follow, but unfortunately it doesn't work that way!" She speaks from experience; to get promoted to her current role Marie-Amélie had to fight.

"I had to ask for what I wanted because in companies most of the women do their job very well, so managers don't want them to move because it's destabilizing for a while." That's one reason why promotions don't come easy, to keep things steady. So when women don't ask for more, managers assume that everyone is happy. If you look at men, they always request what they want and go for it.

In her previous position in Paris, Marie-Amélie was doing a good job, her appraisals were favorable, everyone was happy and wanted her to stay there. They told her it was too early to move, that she had to learn a few more things. Marie- Amélie had other plans. "Yes it's true, I'm not perfect; nobody is. Of course I can still learn more but I said, 'No, I've been doing this job for three years, and I've been doing it well so either you make me move or I'm going to go.'" Tensions rose as the company gave various reasons why she couldn't move. Eventually the company realized that they could lose her.

Around that time Marie-Amélie received an offer from another company. With a strong leverage and backup she went back to management and said, "I love my job, my colleagues and the company; I don't want to move and there's still a lot more I can contribute but come on, other people believe I can do this job so why don't you just give me a chance to do it? I'd rather do it with you guys since I've been here for three years than with someone else so how can we work this out?" Finally, it worked out.

It's an incredible story because a lot of women wouldn't have negotiated like that, they would have just left. It took great conviction and fearlessness from Marie-Amélie who knew she didn't want to leave the company but at the same time was ready to accept the consequences in order to move on to the job that she really wanted. "Working in an inspiring atmosphere is like a relationship, whether love or friendship, it has its ups and downs and is hard work," she explains. "Some moments it's difficult but you don't want to give up. Sure the grass may be greener on the other side but not always. Let's try to make it work first before we part."

Having a bullish personality and not being afraid of taking risks can definitely help a woman win her battles, but mostly Marie-Amélie credits her behavior to her belief in fate. She says that whatever happens is meant to be – if, after pushing, things still don't move then she'll take a different direction.

### Selling Sugar and Moving to Mexico

Fresh out of business school, Marie-Amélie moved to Mexico to breathe some new air as she felt the need to move away from Paris. She had some friends in Mexico but didn't speak any Spanish and lacked job leads. She wasn't quite sure what she would do. Just a few days after arriving, she met the general manager of the cosmetic company Guerlain, who coincidentally was looking for a Frenchwoman to replace the marketing manager. Despite having no experience in marketing, she became a desirable candidate, not only because she was

French but also because she had a background in business that would enable her to work on the projects they were targeting. The pay was miserly, but she wasn't in the position to negotiate.

She still marvels at the great chance and trust given to her at the tender age of 23, but she explains that it wasn't just a matter of luck. Something on her resume singled her out. As a student she had worked one summer for a sugar company selling sugar to supermarkets. No one wanted that job because it required considerable car travel, covering the large Parisian suburbs and waking up at 4am every morning to get to the supermarkets in time to do the merchandising before opening hours. "Sugar is the worst thing to sell," she says. "You have no added value compared to your competitors. You have no specific quality with your product. It's like you are selling petrol. It's a raw material." So when the GM from Guerlain saw that on her resume – and it was impossible to not notice as the only thing on it – he praised her courage, stamina and guts and handed her the job at the company.

**Steadfast Support**

Courage, stamina and guts are what have continually moved Marie-Amélie forward. Before negotiating with the current company and putting herself in an uncomfortable situation, she had only relied on her own instinct and a few words exchanged with her husband. If it's true that behind every great man there is a great woman, then for Marie-Amélie even the opposite is true, counting her husband as her number one supporter. Although he may still be the main breadwinner in the family (he is a partner at a top management consulting firm), he didn't hesitate to take a professional risk to follow his wife to Hong Kong. "That's very strong support and I don't know many people who have that," she says. Just the day before our interview her husband told her he was sure she'd go a long way in her career. "When someone believes in you so strongly it's easier to be confident and feel strong enough to go for things," she adds.

Some years back while doing her MBA she attributed the reason to her success to her husband and his support. Quite often, she says, women have to work harder, and when they are the only woman in a room filled with men they always have to find where they fit in, something that is not necessarily easy.

Actually it's a common 'secret' among successful women CEOs to have strong support from their husbands or another close family member or friend. It would be very difficult to reach those levels by themselves. Men tend to be confident and forthcoming but women are hyper-critical of themselves which becomes the reason they don't push enough to advance in their careers. Many women don't really believe they can succeed.

But not everyone is so fortunate to have strong support readily available, so an idea would be for those women to find a mentor within their network or hire an executive coach. Of course if you are just beginning your professional life it may be difficult to afford a coach, says Marie-Amélie. But once you start reaching senior management positions it is good to see a coach once or twice a month as he or she can help you ask the right questions of yourself and keep you aligned with what you want to do. Marie-Amélie, for example, has a coach to help her when she has to make difficult decisions. At work, being the one in charge, she is often alone in making decisions and managing the business. Without anybody else at her level in the organization, it can be a daunting task to make the right decision. "You can't talk to your boss because he assumes that you are strong enough to make your own decision but sometimes you have your doubts," she says. Another way to use a coach is to discuss what kind of manager you are, such as noticing where you are coming on too strong or how you can spur your people to grow. “What it does is pull your head out of the water to see a different perspective,” she says.

With regard to personality, it is essential to accept that it can be difficult being in an uncomfortable zone. As Marie-Amélie says, people by nature don’t like to feel uneasy. The idea is that things need to get worse before they get better. If you avoid facing certain issues, they will stop you from advancing. Philosophically, Marie-Amélie believes that from bad situations, something good will always result; this has proven true for her in the past. Ironically it is also true that you learn much more from difficulty so one could go so far as seeing adversity as a blessing!

### Women at the Top

Recent numbers show that in Hong Kong only about 8% of women are represented at executive levels of Fortune 500 companies, while at lower levels there are almost as many women as men. According to Marie-Amélie, the simplest answer to this phenomenon is that most women don't want the highest positions. They are happy to work hard early in their careers but once they reach 35-to-40 years of age, when it's time to really hit the turbo button, most women walk out of the race and either give in to motherhood and/or pick less demanding career roles. On this point, we don't agree with Marie-Amélie because we feel that the reason most women walk out of the race at that age is not because they want to but because it is simply impossible for them to manage the new pressures required to move up the ladder, in conjunction with the demands of motherhood. This feeling is particularly acute in a work environment that values face time over other factors.

However, Marie-Amélie has a point: some women simply may not want to.

We ask her what she thinks should be done to avoid women dropping out of career ascents in their mid-thirties. Her view is that within a company, high-potential women from ages 25 to 30 to 35 should be identified. The next step would be to ascertain whether these women really want to become leaders, keeping in mind that their attitude might also change along the way. To guarantee a smooth journey, the company needs to then make sure that during specific periods of their lives, women are given the flexibility to be out for a number of months, such as during pregnancy, so that they don't feel punished for getting pregnant or for taking maternity leave. If you allow women to be with their babies in the first months without feeling guilty they will come back even more motivated and determined.

It's also important to identify high-potential women because as a company you can't do that for every woman. "Okay, it's unfair, I agree," says Marie-Amélie but she offers to see it as a kind of promotion. Instead of giving a bonus or the next title, the woman employee keeps that job but gets one year off. In the end, both parties benefit because it encourages a long-term invested relationship.

Using flexibility as a bonus is an interesting concept. Since you're going to be a burden to the company during those periods when you need time off, like through maternity, Marie-Amélie says - you can make a company adjust for your well-being. In this sense it is not a financial bonus but a material bonus of comfort, health and support.

Another way of increasing flexibility is to allow women to be home, caring for their kids at dinner time, usually between 6 and 8pm. They can make up for those hours by working again from 10pm to midnight. This is the way Marie-Amélie's 30-year old sister works at the consulting firm McKinsey. She has a little girl at home and is pregnant with her second child but manages to work hard. As long as the job gets done, the company and the clients are both happy. For the employer, it's basically about accepting that women can manage their schedule in a different way from men without making the organization suffer.

"I really don't care if my team manager is at home or at the office, as long as the job gets done. And I know that one day, if there's an important matter we can do it over the weekend, so it's about being responsible," says Marie-Amélie speaking for her own organization. It's also obsolete to have face-to-face meetings all the time when people can conduct them over the phone or via email.

Things are a little more complicated when trying to bring flexibility to travel, but there is still room for improvement in making sure that the schedule isn't as fixed as it is today. There is a choice when it comes to working remotely. The more women reach senior positions, the more they will ensure that this flexibility is possible. "Now, even though there's a woman at the top, the company is run by men so she's surrounded and a lot of things aren't changing. Today's schedule is a man's schedule," she says.

Marie-Amélie however points out that while it's true that it's not easy to reach and be in top leadership positions, because the amount of stress increases, it's also true that once you reach those levels there are some perks too, which include a higher level of flexibility.

"What needs to change is the way people work together and interact," she observes. "Employers should allow time off-work to people who need it without making them feel guilty because ultimately that's what makes them quit. And I mean quitting from moving up, not from their job – so if you remove this guilt, then you'll have many more women who want to move up. Right now it's too much."

Being very cold blooded, Marie-Amélie discloses that from the company's point of view they don't see the added value in having more women. Businesses run quite well as they are already, so why bother changing? Even women have become convinced that they don't bring more margin or market share or higher productivity. "Women today don't want it and even if they want it, they feel they aren't able to do it. They aren't supported, pushed, helped, so they feel very lonely and very guilty" says Marie-Amélie. On this last point we completely agree.

But companies should look at this matter a lot more seriously, she notes. Right now the human workforce is reducing after the most recent baby boom so some companies are going to lack quality human resources, as there will not be enough men to replace all the people that will retire a few years from now. The only way forward will be to hire women. With this real need arising soon, companies, for their own interest, should start grooming their female talent because whether they like it or not, the landscape is going to change. To see the future, we just need to turn our heads to China where women entrepreneurs are becoming increasingly successful. Another push at some point will come from stock holders who will become more concerned with gender-equality ratios. At that point CEOs of high-profile companies will have no choice but to make the change in favor of their women index. And some companies have already started to take the lead.

So the only question left is when, not if, it will happen. Implementing a fixed quota for women could make it happen sooner. Most people are of two minds about this, with the worst critics fearing that this will bring inept women to the top. This isn't an issue, says Marie-Amélie, for to reach a certain level means that that particular woman already must be good – not to mention that there are many incapable men as well – so basically the quota wouldn't make any difference.

### Setting Up a Business

In her mid-twenties, after leaving Guerlain, Marie-Amélie was still in Mexico and hadn't quite clicked with her new job, so she set up her own business selling luxury handicrafts from Mexico to Europe. After the first couple of years, she knew that to grow her business she had to find a partner to bring some capital, knowledge and help. Not the setting up but the growing of the business had become the difficult part. She was aware that, around the third year of business, most small companies go bust. She also realized that sustaining and developing the growth requires different skills, attitudes and a whole new business plan. On her own she was sure to fail, so for months she looked for a partner but didn't find any serious candidates. In the end she sold the business and returned to Paris.

"It wasn't an easy decision and luckily it wasn't a failure, but I thought that not finding a business partner was a sign. On top of this, after four years in Mexico I was still single and it was very difficult for me to find someone there because all the foreigners were already with someone and I was too independent for Mexican guys." That's when she realized that if she wanted to find a life partner it wasn't going to happen in Mexico. So she entered an MBA program back in France and within six months met her husband.

What's interesting is that a lot of women these days leave corporate firms to start their own business in order to get that flexibility that they couldn't attain as an employee. Instead Marie-Amélie did the contrary and with that experience behind her, is more than happy to be an employee. The first obvious advantage is receiving a regular salary and also not having to deal with a lot of mundane details.

"What is there not to like about speaking daily with the CEO of one the biggest companies in the world in my industry, tackling very challenging business situations, travelling extensively and dining at great restaurants?" asks Marie-Amélie. We agree with her that it all appears to be very rewarding. Taking the idyllic images out of entrepreneurship and leaving you with the hard truth is consistent with her style. She explains that if she were to create her own business tomorrow, she would be most likely packing boxes and dealing with IT problems. Being an employee rather than an entrepreneur also means that you can sleep at night because you don't have the pressure and anxiety of dealing with the fact that if people don't pay you, that's your food and you can't pay your own employees. Of course, Marie-Amélie conceded that being an employee might never make you a millionaire, like some successful businesses could, but it can still be exciting and is a less troublesome road.

Still today, like most women, Marie-Amélie has plenty of ideas for startups but she is nowhere close to making the leap, knowing well what it costs and unwilling to sacrifice her well-being and comfort. Just imagine if she hadn't had that experience early on, she might have been more ready to jump in even now. "Maybe in 10 years' time if I get bored of the big corporate world I'll do it again, but now my priority is to start a family."

In the meantime she has just signed a contract that will keep her in Hong Kong for another couple of years. After an abrupt beginning, things have been smooth albeit a little fast sometimes for Marie-Amélie who interestingly compares Hong Kong people's instinctive business sense to the French strategic one.

And as a Frenchwoman herself, her own ascent in the business world hasn't been a fluke. "Since I was very young I knew I wanted to be very successful in my business life. I wanted to make the difference, be recognized in what I would do. And since I started working I've always wanted to be at the top. That was my motivation. Maybe I'll make it, maybe not," concludes Marie-Amélie who says part of her strength comes from the people who have believed in her. You might know what you are good at but as someone said to her, "You can only see yourself in two-dimensions but others see you in 3D." So sometimes you may think you are good at things but others don't and vice-versa. It is also good to be aligned with what you want to do and what people think you can do, that's why being supported helps to achieve the objectives.

Recently Marie-Amélie set herself a new personal challenge: to run a 25-kilometer race on the demanding Hong Kong trail. She started training four months before the event and in a typical week was running 40 km, waking up at 6am daily to go running. It was tough to wake up that early and especially keeping up with the training and then go to work, or keeping it up while on holiday in India. "But on the day of the race when you achieve your goal, and I did a good time, you feel amazing," she admits. "It was so empowering. Life is like that. You go through months when you push yourself really hard and then you balance it out with other months. I believe everyone can have it all, whatever that all means, but not necessarily at the same time because you can't do everything at 100%. There are ups and downs, and it's just the flow of things that we have to accept and look forward to while holding in our minds our long-term vision."

# Chapter 7
# Passion
# Yana Peel

*After starting her career in finance, Yana Peel followed her instinct and dove into the art world where her connections with corporate institutions have allowed her to make a big splash. Guided by **PASSION** she has become a leadership model for anyone who wants to contribute in an original and transformative way.*

It's hard to keep up with Yana Peel. Upon meeting her, a steady flow of thoughts come out of her in quick succession. Her eyes sparkle with excitement as her head nods emphatically to drive home each idea. It's our first meeting of the morning but on our way up to Grey Café at The Upper House, we spot her in an orange leather jacket speaking animatedly on the phone from a corner in the hotel lobby. Judging by the time, it might very well be someone in another time zone on the line, a potential participant for one of her many philanthropic projects.

As the co-founder and director of Outset Contemporary Art Fund, she initiates and oversees projects backing the education, production and display of contemporary visual art, mainly by raising funds to support leading museums, public galleries and stimulating art events. As a result of her influence she sits on the board of various art organizations from London to Moscow to Hong Kong. In the past two years alone, she's been awarded numerous international recognitions that underline her professional achievements and her commitment to society.

At any given time she says she's got fourteen things going on. "I just like to organize," she says with understatement. "I'm not an artist, not a poet, not a writer, not a filmmaker. I can't produce art but I am creative in my head and it's a kind of creativity that is very structured." In 2003 she left Goldman Sachs after working there for seven years. During that time she covered three different roles: she set up the emerging markets desk in 1997, two years later she set up e-commerce, and finally in 2001 she moved to hedge fund work. Naturally she's always had a special knack for new ideas and projects. In fact, compared to the very focused people who can have great professional relationships for decades, she's the kind of girl who, barely awake, scans 72 tweets and four newspapers, hungry for information and new stimuli.

That's been the light guiding her throughout her career so far. There was never a master plan; all simply evolved by answering a personal voice that steered her around specific ideas, art and politics. In her latest project, Yana is the producer of *Art for Baby*, a book of artworks (from renowned international artists) that were specifically created to stimulate toddlers' early appreciation for art.

Born in Russia, she grew up in Canada, lived in London then went back to Russia again before moving to Hong Kong with her husband and two young boys. Other than drinking heaps of coffee, Yana cites a peculiar remedy that helps her recharge her batteries: "People relax me. For years, building Outset was about doing our work during the day, putting the kids to bed and going out with artists all night." People would ask Yana if she was exhausted and she'd reply that if she was exhausted she wanted to be around people because that's how she got energy. And when she's not with people, she's on the phone with them, racking up the craziest mobile phone bills.

In a way, Yana is part of that large group of women who drop out mid-career from high intensity corporate jobs. The reasons can vary greatly, but quite often it's a mixture of all the reasons put together. For some the main motive is the desire to spend more time with their kids; some have great business ideas; some just want a more flexible lifestyle. For Yana it was mostly a higher calling that made her leave. She says: "I wanted to go into the arts; I wanted to create a whole different universe," which she's done so far but doesn't rule out the chance of returning to the corporate world in the future. "A woman's life is so cyclical that it doesn't stop when it stops, there are so many phases."

Her seven years in the corporate environment were very positive. She speaks fondly of the nurturing, inspiring and wonderful people she met along the way. In fact she says finance is a good launch pad from which to continue a long corporate life or go on to other things. "It's a wonderful place to start because it gives you structure, accountability for finishing projects," she says. "If you get into art, you are making a financial sacrifice and I wasn't in that kind of situation where I could make a sacrifice." Finance is certainly among the best-paid industries coming out of school and it allows one to surround herself with smart people. At the moment, however, Yana is working with a lot of artists who confront messy situations in which no responsibility is being taken toward a well-defined end goal. Her word of advice for anyone just starting out amounts to this: "No matter what you do, no matter how creative you think your ambitions are, unless you are an artist, there have to be performance indicators: 'What is a success? What is positive? What is your deadline?'" So if you had just come out from university and wanted to become an artist, down the line you wouldn't benefit from all the connections made otherwise you wouldn't have the understanding of how a system works, she says.

What Yana was doing at Goldman Sachs and what she is doing now are not actually that different. The common theme has always been to gather people around interesting ideas, creating new products and filling gaps in the market. At the moment, with half her career spent in the corporate world and the other half in philanthropy, it has become obvious that her time in finance enabled her to reach the second stage. "I've been so fortunate because what I've built is having a voice between two worlds by bringing private people and corporations into the arts," Yana concedes. "It is quite amazing because it takes a certain confidence and ability to talk to different kind of people."

**Women at Work**

"Single people are more efficient," declares Yana referring to the sizeable amount of work you can get done if you don't have limitations with your time. Even so, people with families perform well in fulfilling jobs. It's really just a matter of finding the most suitable environment for each person's needs. For Yana, it was moving into a more flexible working style. "I think I am working more hours and much harder now than I ever did in my life, but I can wake up at 5am and go for a run or I can work on Skype at 2am. It's a whole different time management."

She continues, "If you tell working mothers they have to work 10 to 12 hours a day for a firm, they can do that but they need more flexibility in terms of when those hours are going to be spread out during the day."

Expanding on the non-linear ways in which women operate, Yana adds, "For example, five of those hours might be from 9pm and 2am, which is the way I work at the moment. The challenge is when you have to work those hours in the compliance of a market place or an office because your colleagues need to see you doing that work."

Some companies such as her past employer have a return program through which they try to bring talented women back to the workplace after maternity by offering them more flexible packages.

For Yana, the best solution is to check out of the traditional work environment when you determine it's best for you and then return 100% only when you're ready. "The blanket is only so long: either your feet or your head sticks out," she explains. "If you are going to be the best you can be in the corporate environment you have to work those hours that your peers are working to gain their respect and be there for the clients, so I think it's challenging to rise through the ranks and expect an organization to work on your own time." At the moment there's a better model than in years past for people who leave for a time, but she says it's always difficult to have to make those choices.

Of all places, Hong Kong is without doubt one of the most accommodating cities that enable you to have it all (or nearly all). The support system here is very strong; if you don't have family members on call then you can easily hire someone to help you at a relatively low price. In comparison, in the United Kingdom, one may not have a choice because it costs more to hire a nanny than to go out and get a job. A lot of women in those situations prefer to stay home with their children than spend all their salaries in expensive childcare. This scenario imposes long-term costs, however, as it is then difficult to return to a professional career after a total break.

"If I didn't have children, I would gladly work 14 hours a day back at Goldman or in a museum, so for me the challenge is that there are hours a day I choose to devote to my family - to which my husband doesn't feel he has to devote to as rigidly during the week," Yana says. She mentions a great TED.com video by Facebook COO Sheryl Sandberg on 'Why we have too few women leaders,' (you should see it if you haven't already). In her 15-minute talk Sandberg attributes the reason women are hitting the glass ceiling to three main points: they don't believe in themselves, they don't have equal partners at home and they start adjusting their lives for a baby way too early. The pressures are so great for women that in the workplace in the United States two-thirds of married men have kids while only one-third of married women have kids: a dynamic that isn't sustainable in the long run. But the most shocking news for women comes when Sandberg unveils a study that illustrates how successful women aren't as likeable as successful men. They just aren't the people you want to hang out with. Blame it on traditional perceptions of society or on successful women who pick up the worst male traits to get to the top; at the moment all this paints a rather grim picture for any woman who may harbor lofty aspirations.

Back to Sandberg's three main points – while the first one, "believe in yourself," is very important and self-explanatory, the second one," make your partner an equal partner," aims to alleviate pressure at home. Sure, many of us may have been brought up in very traditional households, but if you do want to work and have kids, then you'll have to delegate some of the household and childcare obligations to your partner. See it as striking a contemporary balance.

Finally, and this is the most interesting and trenchant point of Sandberg's talk, women shouldn't think about adjusting their life to kids until they have kids. What happens is that way before even finding a husband, a woman is thinking of ways to work less to carve out that necessary time to give to a future family. The problem is that this puts them out of the game from the start, which in turn doesn't give a woman the incentives and exciting challenges that a job can give you as you advance. Of course if a woman already knows she doesn't want to work after starting a family, that's fine. But if she does want to keep on working then she has to keep both feet in the game. There is no doubt men more often have this concentrated focus even when they are planning for a family.

From the network of current and former Goldman Sachs women employees, Yana has noticed how most ladies already have ideas of what they want to do later, after their current job. In a way it's an essentially female trait to have lots of marvelous business ideas and an eye on the next big thing. But on the other hand, unless they are serious about implementing them, then just daydreaming takes away the focus from her current job. Yana hypothesizes that, if speaking to a group of male analysts, they would probably just want to do their job and play rugby on the weekend.

**Global Force**

When Yana arrived in Hong Kong three years ago she didn't have a platform or an idea of how Outset would translate into a community that didn't have museums you could fund with private patronage. Now with Outset, she is bringing different projects to the region through their involvement with Para/Site, a non-profit art organization for which Yana sits on the board. She catalyzed a group of friends around Para/Site in a model of cultural philanthropy. For example, the children's book she published was launched at the Louis Vuitton exhibition space in Tsim Sha Tsui, where they did a show with contemporary artists Takashi Murakami and Damien

Hirst. Then the money she got through the sales of the book was put somewhere else to fund another project. A cycle perpetuates. "So, rather than involve the model that we have in the UK, where you each give out twenty thousand in a pot and with that money I go a buy an artwork for a museum," she explains. "Here the model has been about doing projects that generate funding that I can then re-channel because I don't think the community here is yet ready to give collectively into a pot."

Yana also sits on the board of the Hong Kong Art Fair (HKArt) which has gathered momentum since its inception only a few years ago. In this role, Yana has thought to make the exposition more meaningful by bringing some content that didn't exist. As with Outset where they have been bringing people to artist's studios, to meet curators, to see museums, off the beaten track, in that same way she thought, "Why don't I bring an off-the-beaten track discussion to a very popular environment?" For the first fair, via Intelligence Squared Asia, yet another of Yana's ventures, she brought a thought-provoking debate and heavyweight personalities such as David Tang and Colin Renfrew. With an audience of 600-plus she managed to create another platform. In the following fairs the debates evolved to talk about democracy and this past year whether "Art must be beautiful" with controversial artist David LaChapelle among the featured debaters.

So she's done all this in only three years in a new city but what she is most proud of is doing it all while having a baby. During the last HKArt she was nine months pregnant and in perfect timing gave birth four days later. "I also won the Montblanc prize for culture philanthropy in the UK and it was wonderful to be able to give that funding back to the community, so that's what we are doing: we bring corporate and privates where they didn't know they wanted to be."

For someone who says, "Women can do it all but not all the time," Yana is doing pretty well. Of course the flexibility she enjoys in her creative field is not comparable to women who are in finance, law or politics. But then she has worked hard for it with her intelligence and entrepreneurial flair. We can't help but consider this model of working and living as a new evolution of work style, which – thanks to women - is more attuned to the needs of family and environment.

Gone are the days when Anson Chan was starting her career; so much has changed. What are the challenges that modern women face? "Wanting to be everywhere all the time and to do everything," says Yana. "It's not the glass ceiling that holds women back. My experience has showed me that women are not bound by any limitations apart from the ones that they place upon themselves. Then ask me in ten years and maybe it will be different."

Yana is definitely driven but her femininity is evident in her style as well. We ask how she got to where she is today. "I work really hard," she says simply. "For six years my partner and I did it by ourselves. We had no team, but now we have a team of four." So the most important thing is to be surrounded by wonderful people, whether it is an equally driven partner or assembling the kind of great team that Yana has now.

# Chapter 8
# Strength
# Catherine Bradley

*Just like other successful women, Catherine makes her rise to the top sound like a breeze, while raising three children and staying married to the same person. Sure, she has a sense of vocation and loves her specialty, but at her core are a natural rebelliousness and indomitable* ***STRENGTH****. Now with her influence, she hopes to impart her experience to young women and inspire them to become the new leaders of tomorrow.*

"It's a jungle out there," she says candidly, sitting up straight with her mid-length blond hair falling neatly behind her shoulders and her elbows resting on the table in front. Meet Catherine Bradley, currently Managing Director and head of the Equity Linked Solutions Group Asia Pacific at Credit Suisse. "That's why we have too few women in executive roles. Women often think they can get to the top of the corporate ladder by being very good intellectually but what it takes really is a whole new set of skills. There's always someone ready to climb higher and faster and stick you where you belong, so you have to quickly learn how to adapt and fend for yourself in the new environment."

Her own ascent wasn't devoid of sticky situations. Catherine was born and educated in Lyon, France, but she started her career in the US. One day, after about one month on the job, she found herself cornered in the lift by a gang of women bankers in suits and bowties, (a vision from the set of Melanie Griffith's *Working Girl*). "You're not playing by the game," they said. Perplexed Catherine asked for further explanation. "You are dressed inappropriately." In her chic Parisian attire – blazer and mismatched pencil skirt – she no doubt stood out from the troop of women dressed in unflattering pant suits. Those were the days when to succeed in the US it was necessary to look like a man.

Catherine, however, wasn't the type to give in easily; she just brushed those comments aside and that day decided she'd never be like those women clones. "'I'm going to be myself, I'm going to have kids, I'm going to be feminine, I'm going to succeed in my own way," Catherine recalls telling herself. "That has dictated my whole life; I didn't follow a stereotype but I just got on with it, not worrying about the 'woman way' of doing things." In any case, there was hardly any model of successful senior woman to copy or aspire to.

From the very beginning she learned how to follow her own instinct. Coming from a well-established provincial medical family, she was the only one who dared not to pursue medicine and moved instead to Paris to study international finance. While all her relatives are settled in Lyon, she went to New York on a graduate training program, then relocated in her mid-twenties to London where she met her English husband, and has steadfastly maintained the same international path. She attributes her success in business not so much to her ambition but to her refusal to adopt the conventional way – she relishes difference. She concedes that to get out of the model of your whole youth takes a strong personality that not everybody has.

An audit in Catherine's company showed that senior women in banking usually cover back-office and shared services jobs, not revenue-generating and client-facing roles. In fact the trend shows that most women leave the bank (Catherine stressed that this is clearly an industry fact, not specifically her company) after reaching the VP level, at around 28 or 29 years old. So it seems that not enough women are able to navigate the hostile terrain that obstructs the route above VP or middle management. It is the same story all over the world and in different industries to varying degrees.

As a result of this audit Catherine decided to take all the women from the investment banking department in Singapore out to lunch. From the recently joined analyst to the most senior person, there were about a dozen women in all. During the outing, Catherine brought up the issue about women leaving banking careers and what she found out was that to those women there were better options elsewhere. Women are happy to forgo success and high salaries, as well as elevated stress and lack of personal time, in exchange for something else. Getting married and starting a family is generally still expected in many Asian cultures, she heard; even though fewer women are committing to marriage in Asia as reported by The Economist in September 2011. According to Catherine, women in the banking world are not maximizing their full potential. "Maybe it's that a lot of women just trust too much that the system will look after them, don't do enough personal PR and maybe it's humility…" she trails off. Clearly, it's not that easy to say.

The risk is that when a woman doesn't get what she wants or needs from the company, she still stays because she is afraid of destabilizing her family setup; then she can plateau and turn sour. That is when other colleagues start to label a woman as being "emotional" or "difficult" and this makes organizational life even harder for that woman. On the other hand, strong personalities in women are usually criticized in her peer group whilst for men strong personalities tend to be treated with reverence and awe, if not fear.

**Looking Through The Glass**

Catherine believes that one of the elements women are missing is the ability to see the way that they can move to a higher level of influence. She finds that many male bankers can already visualize themselves moving up to the next level while women tend to need the reassurance that they are doing a great job in their current role. It seems that they don't see the next job or that they feel inadequate to seek the next move. Men in banking, in contrast, will more often just "go for it".

And by further comparison, women in banking are fewer in number and therefore less supported. It is, in fact, a hermetically sealed world. A woman could lack in ambition but then just by interacting with other women with higher aspirations she could be inspired. But there are very few women that share similar positions and problems so they don't have many points of reference. By contrast, men stick together and have much more social contact with peers as well as a support net to fall into or bounce off. This helps men to collaborate inside and outside the office (the after-work drinks ritual is a great bonding platform). But women may have to build their initiatives in greater isolation; the ability to win peer group support for promotion is correspondingly much lower. If a man fails it's okay because he has his buddies to fall onto but a woman is more likely to be ostracized.

Another factor is that women could also be nicer to each other. There is always this competition factor that can be traced back to school days. It's a quality that can bring out the worst in women. "Men seem to learn how to be better at disguising rivalries or at brokering "working arrangements".

Yet another shortcoming for women in Catherine's world is that they tend not to make a distinction between themselves and their job. Several times when male bankers have walked out of a meeting room after making a weak presentation or losing a mandate, they would distance themselves and joke: "My pitch was not fantastic, but I'm good". Whereas many a woman striving to compete may invest everything she's got into a pitch or a deal, so in the face of criticism or failure she thinks she's all bad and alone.

Catherine explains, "In fact most women in banking at my level, who really made it, and on a lasting basis, tend to be married, maybe with kids. It could simply be that we're compelled to switch off once we get home and we don't take setbacks so seriously because we have another life that helps to give us a better perspective. It's sad to see that many of the single women burn out despite being brilliant". And it's ironic what Catherine says, that it would be the mundane activities of home and family – that most women feel they have to sacrifice in order to succeed – that preserve successful women from taking everything too personally.

The fact that fewer women who stay in banking are marrying or having kids is disconcerting. For ambitious women it's difficult to find the right partner because other than having too little free time to date they have been ingrained with the idea that they have to 'marry up' to men who are more educated or financially or socially successful than they are.

Catherine herself got married at 25 and had her first child two years later which is quite young for a promising star in banking. Perhaps she was lucky to have met the right person early on because as the earning power grows so does the intimidation factor. "I see successful women that frighten men," she says. "They are too independent and critical and they don't realize it." Catherine had her ideas straight from the onset: she was not going to marry a lawyer, banker or accountant; in her case, she married an architect. "Two very ambitious people in a couple, in the same line of business is a risky combination," she says. "You need someone who has a different mindset and values to help you switch off and relativize. Many couples in banking fail because it's just too difficult."

**Rise to the Top**

"I've been lucky because I love what I do," says a grateful Catherine. "I am well-known in Europe, the US and now in Asia for being highly specialized in my industry: I'm the equivalent of a neurosurgeon, brought in by other practitioners to solve a complex issue with high- profile transactions," she adds. Her ability to develop a large network and to broker complex technical solutions between clients, regulators and traders, and to create solid teamwork between disparate internal departments, has been the reason for her success. Sure, she's had some difficulties getting to the top, but her strong technical knowledge has always given her a huge jolt. Then when she suffered setbacks she had to go home anyway and make sure the nanny was not resigning and the clothes were dry.

Catherine has three children, or rather she says "three times one child", spread over 11 years; a big gap but it was the only way to focus on each child in turn, since she was traveling all the time. Even so, it was really tough sometimes. After delivering her first child, she was back at work in less than a week: At that time she was at Merrill Lynch where she suddenly landed a prestigious mandate. So she was unexpectedly asked to fly to Paris to work on its execution out of a hotel for four weeks: no time to wean her baby who stayed in the UK. She arrived in a rush to her first presentation to find at the entrance of the room that her silk blouse was stained with dripping milk. She lightly supports her forehead with her fingers and ruefully remembers the awful episode in her past, pointing out how silly and too eager to please everyone she was.

As the children grew, so did Catherine's responsibilities at work, requiring even more of her time out of office hours. It certainly wasn't easy and she suffered from this loss of precious time as she loves being with her kids. Still, she felt no pangs of guilt. Many mothers are consumed by guilt at leaving their precious children in the hands of nannies. Catherine instead says she was lucky to have been educated by a partly working mom (a dentist) so it was natural for her to work, too. She adopted her own way to check if her presence at home was sufficient: If her kids still managed to be bilingual from her in spite of her never being home, while living in England and going to English pre-school, then her mission was accomplished and it meant that somehow, somewhere, she was doing something okay.

Even today with all kids away at boarding school or college, all of her free time is dedicated to her kids, her husband and her home – and she makes sure that time is devoid of any kind of Blackberry fiddling and work-related distractions. She pulls out a piece of paper from her bag reminding her to go to the gym. She shows it to us then crumples it up together with her resolution to exercise. "I never manage to have any time for myself, I don't have any hobbies!" she exclaims. Instead she mentions shortcuts to buy time. She bought a scooter "because it is the quickest way to be home in time for the cherished bedtime, or to beat traffic and pop in midafternoon for the school's Christmas carol performance or a child's medical check-up, before returning to work".

Catherine thinks that watching her children develop with their own personality has also helped her to be a strong and caring manager, and vice-versa, sharing her days with young colleagues and witnessing their centers of interest has helped her relate and adapt best to her growing teenagers. She is also proudly savvy about mobile phones are deemed 'cool' and good for one's 'street cred'.

**Connecting the Dots**

"I see people trying to compartmentalize being a business woman and being a mother," observes Catherine. "In my case, I have everything in my Blackberry, I've never been able to separate my two lives and I never feel bad if my daughter calls me when I'm with clients." In the same way she has always made it clear at work that she had priorities at home. But she never felt comfortable to do the sneaking out, coat over the chair trick, the Friday afternoon 'meetings' out of the office. She did exactly what men do when men go to play squash and it's all fine. One day, while she was working in an open-plan-floor at Merrill Lynch before flexible working became commonplace, she turned to her assistant and announced very audibly "Every week, I will work one afternoon from home. When clients call, can you please transfer them to my mobile?" Many women would never dare to do that, says Catherine. Again it's a hypocritical and unfair social double standard. Because when a man says he has to go home and take care of his child, the whole office thinks: "Oh, what a dedicated dad!" So women just need to do the same and they need to feel happy about it without any sense of guilt.

## What Companies Can Do

A number of companies are implementing diversity policies that look good though they don't always work. Catherine was assigned a colleague mentor when she first arrived in Hong Kong for her current job three years ago. She was also selected last year for an excellent Credit Suisse executive program, which gave her the opportunity to meet twice with members of Credit Suisse Board. Companies are genuinely trying to improve the gender disparity. There are mentoring programs that aim to create stronger bonds between women and men inside the company, but often those relationships are artificial and some individuals may find it patronizing that they are given a mentor just because they are a woman; and they feel that even if they got the promotion, people will snigger for how it was given. So it's a bit of a vicious circle right now.

Could it help to implement a "40%" policy like Norway did, which regulates how many women should be on boards? Catherine is ambivalent. While she agrees with some newspaper articles that consider this reverse discrimination, she also believes that introducing it temporarily to "pump-prime" the system for a while could bring positive results and critical mass so that women can learn from each other. Catherine has noticed that the mere fact of having one, or even better, two women sitting at the table in a meeting room, already makes a difference in the atmosphere. But in reality most men don't quite know how to deal with this change; things will not change just by having women attend more seminars on leadership.

Possibly if women were better at networking they would have higher chances to understand the inner workings of their company. But at big internal events and conferences it becomes apparent how women instinctively tend to go hang out with each other. "Maybe they feel safer but they shouldn't do that," says Catherine. They should be mixing and meeting as many people as they can. It's possible that, particularly single women in the 20s and 30s, avoid contact because of the sexual tension that may arise. They don't want to be viewed as a flirt. Then there is the opposite too, with beautiful women dressing up to the nines causing a stir among other women who feel they are using the wrong tools to get ahead. It's hard to strike the right balance even when you have the best intentions.

**Playing Like a Man**

"Just the fact that we put women in boxes makes us guilty as well. It tends to come out straight away, immediate personality characterization – either "she's not assertive enough" or "she's difficult to control". Nothing in between. We don't categorize men so much, they are just the way they are; with women, we advise them "you should be more like a man" or "you should use your femininity" or "you should be less emotional". We stereotype women and we don't give them a chance to be themselves. We see them as women before seeing them as individuals." Our guess is that women have to first learn what the "rules of the game" are and become good at playing by those rules before they can change them – because you can't change the rules unless you understand them first. What happens though is that a lot of women who do make it learn the rules but then forget that at the beginning they hated those rules. And they forget that there comes a point when it's time for them to start changing those rules.

We leave our conversation with Catherine with the impression that this successful woman, so direct and likeable, is well-balanced and happy about her life decisions.

# Chapter 9
# Courage
# Junko Nakagawa

*In the midst of her career, Junko Nakagawa made the **COURAGEOUS** move of taking a four-year hiatus, but by keeping connections alive and by making new experiences she ensured a smooth return for herself in the workplace. Throughout her career she has constantly challenged the glass ceiling of corporate Japan and today is ranked in Fortune Magazine as one of the world's 50 Most Powerful Women in Business - and as one of the most powerful in Japan.*

April 1st 2011 was an exciting day for Junko. She became the first female executive managing director and first female CFO of Nomura Holdings. Anywhere in the world this is a big deal; in notoriously conservative Japan this is exceptional. Junko however, had already had a taste for shattering records. In 2008 she became the first female CEO of a Nomura operating company when she took over the reins of Nomura Healthcare. Then, in 2010, she became co-deputy CFO of the group. In this light, with a clearly visible trajectory, her latest post came hardly as a surprise. But her prospects hadn't always been this apparent: some years back, when she took a long break from her career to follow her husband's relocation to Hong Kong, her professional future had become something of a question mark.

Although some women decide to leave a corporate career (usually to spend more time with their children) without any intention to go back, many women think of taking a break for a few years for family or personal reasons with the intention of going back. Most don't, however, because they fear that they won't be able to go back to a worthwhile career path afterwards.

Junko was at a crossroads. She had a tricky decision to make: should she keep working in Tokyo and have a long distance marriage or should she quit her job and follow her husband to a new city?

That the move was to Hong Kong, a key financial hub, made a big difference. Junko had never experienced living out of Japan and she found Hong Kong's international standing rather appealing. Yet, the thought of leaving the satisfaction of her job was daunting; she worried that she would have a difficult time to get her career back on track after taking a break.

Yet she felt that by following her husband to Hong Kong, other than keeping her marriage alive she might benefit from the international exposure: she would have a chance to see how foreign businesses operated in one of the largest financial cities in Asia. She decided that the benefits of moving to Hong Kong would outweigh the alternative of staying in her job in Japan. She knew she wanted to go back to finance after this break and she knew this was a once-in-a-lifetime opportunity: she was ready to take a risk to boost her career and keep her marriage strong.

"Of course I didn't want to lose my career," recalls Junko of that pivotal time in her life. "But I couldn't choose both. I think the most important thing is to decide what is best for you at the time. Work-life balance is very difficult to define. I don't think it necessarily means 50-50 always. The important thing is to choose what is best at the given moment. " Her strict self-discipline led her to stick to her instincts, so she moved to Hong Kong and never looked back.

In the new city she enjoyed herself with her family and made new friends. "Seeing the diversity of Hong Kong's culture and people was quite interesting," she says and adds that the caliber of financial professionals she met and the vibe of the financial city were also enlightening. In retrospect she confirms that her gut feeling had been right: these new experiences became invaluable to her continued career in finance.

Meanwhile she regularly kept in touch with former colleagues and old friends. She didn't hesitate to ask them for assistance and she always kept a positive outlook on her future career opportunities. For example, she would think back to her early role models at the Asian Development Bank when she first started working part-time as a student. Most of the senior staff had been women, so she'd always thought it was natural for females to be in leading positions.

Also she knew from the past that taking risks pays off. Some years earlier Junko had already come to a crossroads that required a well-pondered decision. Her employer had offered her a new assignment in Nagoya, a city over 250 kilometers from Tokyo, but her husband would not be able to follow her. Was it best to move for the new job or should she stay in Tokyo with her family? After consulting her spouse they decided that for her career, it was best to live apart for some time. The opportunity to gain new experiences in her career was far greater than her prospects in not changing anything at all. She ended up working in Nagoya for nearly three years, during which, as she had anticipated, she amassed some of the most important experiences that still apply to her current job. Again, it was one of the best decisions she could possibly make for her career.

**Early Steps**

As a new graduate from Kobe University, Junko was interested in various areas that ranged from finance to pharmacology and sociology but ultimately she picked finance and joined Nomura, the largest investment bank in Japan. From the start, as a financial advisor, Junko found the job very exciting. Since she was a university student she had always been interested in working in areas related to providing financial services because it would allow her to connect investors and individuals with corporate bodies and institutions through the capital markets. Along the way she participated in numerous stimulating projects, including her involvement in Nomura's conversion to a holding company and its listing on the New York Stock Exchange in 2001. As a key member from Japan on the listing project, she worked very closely with local regulators, lawyers and the relevant parties in the three months leading up to the listing. There wasn't much time for sleep during that period. "It was very intense but I learnt a lot," she says. "Long work hours may sometimes be inevitable but it depends on how you manage your time. Luckily my family has always been supportive."

A crucial step in Junko's career was when she made the transition to investment banking, an area in which historically there had been very few women in key positions. Nonetheless she felt she was given a fair chance. "When I first joined the investment banking division it took me six months to understand all the technical terms. I was worried about whether our clients would accept me as a business partner as there were not a lot of females working in investment banking back in those days." Luckily, there was nothing to worry about. After a short while, Junko was able to manage transactions confidently for her clients.

She adds that her positive attitude and willingness to take on new challenges might have impacted the way she was received by her male peers in investment banking. She ended up staying for eight years before moving into the firm's finance department.

When Junko left her job and moved to Hong Kong with her husband, she was in the middle of a high-flying career. Her experience in successfully taking on great career challenges in her previous years, however, gave her the confidence that she would have been able to go back later on and still be successful.

**Back in Full Force**

So how did she go back? We ask Junko, a little surprised ourselves that after such a long break she was able not only to re-enter smoothly but also to fly to such grand heights. "I kept very strong connections with my former colleagues at Nomura and people in the industry" she replies. "So when my husband and I moved back to Japan, a former colleague asked if I wanted to come back and work for Nomura." Her former company welcomed her back and allowed her to progress professionally from where she had left off.

Junko was extremely smart to keep her connections alive. At the same time, that's an inspiring example of a company that is open to re-accept gifted women, and men, if for some personal reason they need to take some time off. Junko quickly adds that Nomura has been very committed to retaining female talent or talent in general, regardless of gender. Today Dame Clara Furse, former Chief Executive of the London Stock Exchange and a veteran in global financial markets, sits among the board of directors of Nomura Holdings and Chie Toriumi, a senior managing director in the CEO/COO office, is the firm's other female member of senior management together with Junko. And of course, Junko is the first female to become the firm's CFO. While still being a minority, this female representation bodes well for the next generation of women who is already more savvy, prepared, determined and free from dated family constraints.

It's important to place talent at top levels regardless of gender, says Junko, because being a global company means being naturally diverse. Both diversity in the people and diversity in the thinking will help a company build and maintain a competitive advantage. She believes that diversity and inclusion go beyond anti-discrimination or other kinds of policy. It should be a meritocracy that attracts, retains and develops the best people for the right roles and that certainly includes placing talented women in senior positions.

## Practical Support for Women

We ask Junko what other practical programs have been put in place in her company to support women. We learn that to support working ladies, Nomura has a number of practices in place, such as nursing rooms and other forms of support for new mothers and fathers. As we know, most of the time it is the family calling and responsibilities at home that force a woman to feel she needs to quit work. So to better assist parents of young children, Nomura gives employees the option to work six hours a day and be exempt from overtime and holiday work up to the child's third birthday. Also an employee may choose to work two hours less a day until the child's third year of elementary school. These are important options that allow greater flexibility for parents when it is most needed.

With that in mind, we are certain that her company's philosophy has contributed to Junko's rise, while at the same time it was Junko's courage and determination to succeed both in her private life and work that led her to make bold moves throughout her career, including stepping out for a few years, only to come back stronger than ever.

# PART 2

# What We Need To Fight For

# Chapter 10
# Flexibility
# Rainbow Pan

*As CEO of arguably the most woman-friendly company in Hong Kong, Rainbow Pan knows the importance of a good work-life balance. She promotes a family-oriented environment, education, work options and greater **FLEXIBILITY**. As a result she has some of the happiest employees around and very high staff retention.*

Every time her relatives came for a visit in Canton, Rainbow would gawk for hours at the photographs they bore of their adoptive land. Deep blue skies, crystal clear water, iconic architecture of the Sydney Opera House – she found those images of Australia so inviting. It was the 1980s. China's professional landscape was still very rugged compared to that of today; there weren't that many opportunities for many people, let alone a young girl. It didn't take Rainbow, a recent university graduate in economics, too long to make up her mind. One fine day she mustered all her courage, marched up to her mother and announced, "I'm going to Australia."

Her plan was to stay for two years, just enough to get a taste of the Australian way of life. She had already been working for a couple of years in Canton as a business banking manager involved in lending to factories, a career that got off to a very good start. It wasn't unusual in her family, though. She was born into the industry, with everyone on her mother's side in finance. However, the relocation meant that she had to start from scratch as all her previous experience became irrelevant in the new country. Other than a strong cultural divide, there was the inescapable language barrier.

Nothing could deter the young Rainbow. Eventually she joined Westpac bank as a financial planner and years later moved to HSBC as a senior financial planner. Those initial two years quickly turned into 16 years during which both her career and her personal life flourished.

It was a brave move to let go of the familiar and start her career all over again. But Rainbow calls herself a calculated risk taker. For someone like her who'd always known she wanted a thriving career, it was a natural step to take. "To advance in your life, whether it's in your career or other areas, you need to take risks because if you don't, you'll probably stay in your safety zone and you won't get anywhere," she says.

In 2005 she moved to Hong Kong to join ipac, an international financial advising and investment group that helps clients achieve their financial and lifestyle goals. Four years later she became the CEO of the company. Under her reign, in 2010, ipac won the American Chamber of Commerce's Best Company for Women Award. The recognition came at a crucial time as more people took greater notice of gender equality in the workplace. Compared to Hong Kong's nearly equally split workforce, at ipac women make up 69% of the staff. That number rises sharply in the executive band where women dominate with an 86 per cent presence. This is a far cry from the average 8.9 per cent female heads in board positions in companies listed on the Hang Seng Index as reported in 2009 by Community Business, a non- profit organization in Hong Kong that conducts research focused on corporate social responsibility.

ipac retains so much female talent that it nearly appears to be biased in the other direction. "We really don't consider gender, we look at merit and we determine whether the person has his or her mind and heart at work," says Rainbow in reply to our slightly provocative assertion. When it isn't the company to deliberately prevent women from advancing in their careers, the culprit is found in the many small details that add up and become an insurmountable pile of stress to women who have to balance the responsibilities at work with those at home. We could see what companies do – by not increasing flexibility – as an accidental form of "mobbing" to persuade people who can't always commit 100 per cent to quit, leaving the space for another individual who has fewer personal obligations. In Hong Kong, it is not a coincidence that the largest dropout from the workforce comes from women in their 30s, a time when many of them decide to start a family.

Although most corporations acknowledge that it is not only ethically wrong but also a self-defeating business decision to deny women the possibility of competing on equal footing for top posts, women have a practical gap to fill.

For a number of reasons, some cultural and some biological, women are the primary caretakers in a family and for this reason they are playing the corporate game with a handicap. To be sure, women have the choice of competing or not, but wouldn't it be fairer if the playing ground was leveled, thus giving everybody the opportunity to perform at their very best? Unless we want increasingly fewer women to bare children and get married – as is happening in Asia and particularly in China – and we want a smaller talent pool to pick from, companies have the responsibility and the moral duty to ensure that needs of women be met.

Boasting those stellar numbers, ipac must be doing something right to retain that much female talent. To start with, the company openly identifies itself as a family-oriented organization. The official hours are from 8.30am to 5.30pm, which means there isn't a culture of working long hours, unlike in most Hong Kong firms where it isn't abnormal to work until 10pm. "Most of our support staff have family and young children and every year we produce at least a couple of kids," says Rainbow, pointing out the widespread need to work flexible hours to fulfill parental obligations.

When it comes to parenting, Rainbow believes that flexibility does make a difference. When Rainbow gave birth to her daughter (who is now turning 17) in Australia, it was normal to take 12 months off, eight weeks of which were paid and the rest being unpaid leave. "I stayed home until 11 months and I couldn't bear it anymore!" says Rainbow. "I was so bored. I wanted to go to work." So Rainbow returned to the office and her daughter went to long day care. At this stage most women would be suffering pangs of guilt, feeling inadequate as mothers for abandoning their beloved child. Rainbow instead believes it was better for her daughter to get a chance to mix with other kids to develop her social skills and become more independent. Traditionally mothers think they can do a better job at taking care of their own kids. While they can obviously provide a more hygienic environment and make sure the children are safe, at home the kids have less chance to communicate with their peers than at the school. In addition, every day teachers change the setting and arrange different activities so the little ones are constantly having their brains stimulated. Rainbow believes that this contributes to a more well-rounded education for a child.

When it comes to management, Rainbow emphasizes efficiency, yet allows flexibility. At ipac it's perfectly normal to go to work a little later, after dropping kids off at school. Those lost 30 to 60 minutes are then balanced by leaving the office later in the evening or coming in earlier another day. "I'm more focused on efficiency," says Rainbow. "I don't think working long hours necessarily brings in better results. For example, if I have a deadline and it is 9pm and I'm still working, I think that if I don't get some rest, it will impact my work the next day. So I'd rather work very efficiently during the day and focus on productivity."

To have flexible hours also means that some of the staff – particularly the financial advisors who work long hours and often also work on weekends – can manage to fit in a workout routine during the day. As long as they mark it in their diary so that in case Rainbow comes looking for them she knows where they are, then it's okay. In fact, it's important that people in senior positions have that kind of flexibility. When people work long hours and have no recognized flexibility, they are often unable to take care of personal matters so they react by sneaking out, creating issues for both the company and the employee. Explains Rainbow: "Here it's all out in the open with their gyms bags under the desks and their face all red from hot yoga."

This kind of culture seems to have been imported from Australia whose common image gives off a laid-back vibe of people going surfing after work. Rainbow quickly dismisses this as a misconception, citing high-strung working environments, similar to Hong Kong levels, particularly in cities. On the other hand what she did pick up from Australians is her directness in communicating with the staff. "Maybe too direct sometimes," she says.

An added bonus to this kind of flexibility and openness is a higher-than-average staff retention rate. Taking the

Leadership Team as an example, out of the eight staff, seven of them has been with ipac for five years or more. It's not just about managing women but about managing a company well. Happier staff members are unlikely to change jobs, a factor that is very important in a financial advising company built on trust and long-term relationships.

Also, the fact that there are so many women in key positions is very helpful because it means that there is a lot of mentoring from older women to younger ones. There are more role models to look up to. ipac every year does an organization talent review, or OTR. "We talk to each member of our staff and find out what they want to do with their career," says Rainbow. "Sometimes the answer is, 'I want to progress in my current job,' sometimes it's the complete opposite. With all this information we discuss with them what they want to achieve. If what they want is something the company can provide for them, then we will sit down and discuss a development plan in terms of job training, rotation, training courses or we deliberately give them a task to specially train them in that area." She adds, "I think this is very important because through this process we actually identify potential talent. I think people are talented if they put their mind and heart into work and as a company we can motivate them and allow them to grow. The majority of the people in the leadership team have grown within the company."

This kind of ethics is rather impressive. Take Rainbow herself. She started her career as financial planner with ipac. She expressed her ambition to be engaged in the management work in OTR. Gradually, she has progressed to her present position. In another occasion, one of the Client Services Managers has been trained and nurtured to be a Compliance Manager, which is her desired direction of development.

Traditionally the financial planning industry was dominated by men but in the last few years a lot of companies have started recruiting women. Because of their higher sensibility to other people's needs women can relate to different kinds of personalities more easily, making it an advantage to be a woman. They are often also good listeners, which is quite important for the role. It shows somehow that women do possess desirable female traits that enhance performance of a business. Therefore, it's important to nurture female talent in this field.

In Hong Kong ipac also has an educational program called "Women and Money" to help women better manage their lives and finances. Topics include marriage, career, and finance. Other perks include getting a day off on your birthday, a yearly family day and maternity leave that goes above statutory pay allowing for an extended unpaid leave depending on each mother's needs. Again and again, Rainbow and her company put into practice a level of flexibility that works.

# Chapter 12
# Recognition
# Connie Carnabuci

*For 25 years Connie Carnabuci has been at the forefront of the evolution of Intellectual Property. Few topics are as contemporary as this one, let alone as exciting – that is, if like Connie, you happen to love the intricacies of new technology and its effects on society. Also, few people share her expertise, propelling her to be* ***RECOGNIZED*** *as a well-known expert and partners with one of the world's leading law firms.*

As a young girl in high school, Connie's prospects couldn't have been more different. She studied Italian, French and English at a high level and had her mind set on becoming a linguist. That is, until her father, an Italian immigrant to Australia, broke the news to her, remarking, "Honey, you're never going to get anywhere being a translator for the Italians." He suggested she study Japanese instead since at the time, in the late 70s and early 80s, a large influx of Japanese investment in Australia promised golden job opportunities. Disoriented, she jumped back on the carousel of life, hoping to figure out her future by the next stop. It wasn't easy in those pre-internet days; information wasn't widely accessible, making her severely uninformed compared to kids today. Other than the annual trips to visit the "nonni" in Italy, her international exposure during childhood had been quite humble.

Enter her first role model and mentor: an elegant yet unconventional and independent woman in her 40s. She was a modern history teacher who became a great inspiration to Connie. Understanding the girl's predisposition for languages, the teacher steered the teenager toward the study of law.

"What this highlights for me is how important it is for young girls to have people to look up to and that stimulate them," says Connie, now an accomplished lawyer, acknowledging how lucky she was to have met an adult who recognized her strengths and pushed her in the right direction. Connie also had the diligence to excel, earning herself a position in the top 5% of the state in the High School Certificate (HSC) examination. As a result, all higher education doors were wide open and she chose to pursue a double degree in commerce/marketing and law at the University of South Wales.

Upon completion of her degree she was offered a position to be a federal judge's associate which is like a judge's clerkship. However, she did for him the kind of work a junior barrister would do and as time progressed, the judge would start asking her what she thought of each case and how they might decide. In the end, he invited Connie to assist in writing sections of the judgments.

"He was very much about encouraging me to be open, giving me confidence to speak and validating everything I had to say," she says, adding that he was probably her second mentor.

## Joining a Law Firm

Connie became interested in intellectual property which in the early eighties was starting to be a hot topic with the slow rise of the internet. She joined Mallesons' IP department and soon found out it was the right place to be. In 1984 when Philip Argy, one of the head partners at Mallesons and a pioneer in computer law, put a computer on everybody's desk, everyone thought he was crazy. Then when he said that the future was in electronic banking and no one would go to the bank anymore, they started to wonder what he was smoking. But he turned out to be an oracle and throughout her early career, Connie saw his prophecy unfold.

"It was a subject matter that resonated with me," she muses. "When I started we had mainframe computers, then we moved to local area networks, then to wide area networks, then to the internet, so I feel that I've been incredibly lucky because in one career I've watched the technology evolve and the legal issues evolve with the technology, even though legal issues are usually a little bit behind." So far it's certainly been an interesting journey for Connie, whose experience took her all the way through evolving social, economic and political contexts as the law adapted to changes in society. For her, as it would apply to anyone, it was extremely important to be passionate about her job because if she hadn't enjoyed it, when things got tough (and they always do) she could have easily quit, unwilling to deal with the intensity and pressures.

## Building a Family

Somewhere between becoming a partner at Freshfields and moving to Hong Kong, Connie managed to make time to get married and have two children, but the plan hadn't been clear all along. As a university student she was more interested in her professors intellectually than in dating boys her age. While other girls may have sought at university to find a suitable husband, Connie was there merely to learn. She admits to having a few romances here and there, but her number one priority was to work extremely hard. Then, by her mid-20s when all her friends were getting married, she started to wonder if she had made the right choices.

In the meantime, her career kept climbing. At 30, Mallesons offered to relocate her to New York for a couple of years. “It was probably the best two years of my life,” she says. “If I look back at the spikes, it was a major surge in my experience because US firms were doing a lot of the corporate internet-related deals and in those years the internet and email just took off. So again, I was just lucky to be in the right place at the right time.” And of course she made the most out of it. In a city offering limitless things to see and do, she played hard and worked harder. She surrounded herself with nice friends and even got engaged, but didn’t end up getting married, resulting in a personal crisis.

When the New York experience ended, she returned to Sydney. A new client, a major Australian telecommunications player, was launching something called a “portal” and they were going to value the business based on “eye balls” and “ARPU”. Connie knew exactly what those things were and became one of the associates working with the client to launch the telecoms’ giant multimedia platform. On her team, her supervising partner became her next mentor.

“He let me lead, didn’t smother me, didn’t judge the fact that I needed to put on lipstick before a meeting,” she says with gratitude. “He didn’t try to change me, but he trusted me enough to let me do things.” Connie says this partner was important in allowing her to grow and in teaching her the value of not judging people by their appearances but instead by listening to the quality of what they are saying. These are qualities that shouldn't be taken for granted, because more often than not, bosses and supervisors are not progressive and generous in training new talent.

Connie quickly proved that his trust in her hadn't been wasted, as she too when the time came, adopted a similar approach with her team. Perhaps she had been already hardwired to be open to differences. Growing up with a migrant background meant that her family behaved and thought differently from the largely homogenous Anglo-Saxon environment she grew up in. This perspective taught her to appreciate the value of diversity from a very young age.

Her hard work and admirable leadership skills soon paid off as she became a partner of the firm. At that point she had no personal relationship other than with her family, close friends and her little dog named Fifi. Those were dark days of toiling. Then a crack of light started to shine in.

A mutual friend introduced Connie to Paul who had also just returned from New York. With that as a common denominator, their friendship eventually evolved into romance.

Not long after Paul had an opportunity to move to Hong Kong, he asked Connie to join him and be his wife. Thrilled, she accepted both proposals, even though she feared everyone would think she was crazy since she had only been a partner at her law firm for two years.

However, when she told her CEO about the news he was excited as everyone else in the office. He assured her there would be a place for her as a partner in their Hong Kong office.

Connie feels that the fact she met her husband after becoming partner helped her reach a balance in her life.

The two most intense moments of her life – the run to partnership and the strengthening of her relationship and subsequent marriage – came at different times.

Ironically, for most women, those two stages come together, sometimes unsustainably. If it's not marriage, then it is the issue of having babies in one's in mid-to-late 30s, as women delay childbearing in order to first secure successful careers. That kind of clash can be deadly for women's careers. Unable to cope with the mounting pressures and feeling constantly unfulfilled, they quit. For Connie, reaching her highest career milestone before marriage proved the key to success.

**Balancing Act**

With Paul entering the picture for good, Connie had some re-organizing to do. For starters, she wouldn't go into the office on Sunday to organize her desk for Monday. "Like many female lawyers I'm very controlling," says Connie with a smile, so letting go was a conscious effort to change the way she worked and managed herself. Her big learning here was to still do a good job, at a level that was appropriate yet considerate of making time for Paul. "That in crude way was my first attempt to understand work-life balance," she recalls.

All was going well for the newlyweds in Hong Kong, then things got even better. After two years in the new city, the prestigious law firm Freshfields offered Connie to join them. It wasn't an easy decision for her because things were good with her current firm, but she felt that the move would broaden her exposure and grant her an even greater international experience.

During the interview process that lasted almost three months, Connie became pregnant. At 38, six weeks pregnant with her first child, she faced an incredibly tough choice: should she tell her prospective employer? Anything could happen with the pregnancy at that early stage. After much reflection she decided to be open, disclosing her big news to the regional managing partner at the time, a woman, who was sponsoring her entry into the firm.

"Well, that's just a timing issue," the woman replied, taking Connie by surprise. Then everything proceeded as normal, with the firm facilitating Connie's move. More than ever, Connie felt privileged to have dealt with such an amazing person and felt strongly about joining them. It probably made a difference that both her sponsor and the global practice group leader were women.

"So it comes down to being open, but equally if you get a break like that, you can't abuse it," says Connie about returning to work when her son was 12 weeks old. "You then have to come back and deliver." There isn't much she remembers of that first year at Freshfields. She stopped everything and handed the baby over to the helper, not without internal conflicts. And no matter how rough a night she had caring for the baby, she couldn't afford to not show up the next day. "There are sacrifices that you have to make," Connie reminds women. "And you just have to be conscious that you are making those choices and have a good open relationship with your partner."

**Sharing Responsibilities**

Finding Paul was a stroke of luck. Not everybody has a supportive husband who is hands-on with the children to the point that sometimes, as Connie reveals, he might be even better with them than she is. Paul decided to take a career break and for a period of nearly two years, he was at home doing contract work and taking primary care of the children.

"I guess that when you look at a family you have to see it as a comprehensive whole" says Connie. She adds that, now that he's back to full-time work, they've hired a

British nanny because as the children get older parents are needed even more. Children look for a higher level of intellectual and emotional engagement. Other than the primary care, they want to talk about things that upset them, or made them happy.

Back at work, the new firm turned out to be a real meritocracy; much is expected but as much is rewarded too. With about 45 female partners or a 16 percent female representation, Freshfields is on the lower side of the gender equality spectrum, but they are trying to do more, most notably by recently launching a program to retain women longer in the workforce.

As for herself, Connie has come into her own in the new company. Here she can use her own contacts and put her second marketing degree to good use, as the partner sponsor for business development for the region. She is fully satisfied with a functional head role as well as a practice.

Connie attributes her success to a lot of hard work, a lot of luck and some good people along the way who have recognized her potential and given her a chance.

**Attributes of a Leader**

"Some people say you write your own luck, and I write some of that down to my personality, without wishing to sound arrogant," says Connie of her strong emotional quotient and focus on looking forward, concentrating on doing her work properly and not looking over her shoulder worrying about competition or trying to put other people down. In her element, Connie is seen as someone who's trustworthy, who's generous with knowledge, generous with time, all of which make for impressive leadership skills. In fact, as journalist Hanna Rosin mentions in her December 2010 TED talk, "New Data on the Rise of Women", today's desirable leaders aren't intimidating individuals ordering from the top down but all-embracing individuals who can nurture talent and inspire open communication in adaptable environments. These are qualities that are quintessentially feminine. The latest figures show that in the US and in many other countries, women are on the rise in managerial positions because they have the set of skills that are needed in today's workforce. Our numbers here in Asia, except perhaps in China and in India, are still lagging behind.

You can still feel the conflict between women in leadership and authority and being feminine. Some find the answer in behaving like a man, but from what we've seen it's not the best solution. Very few women are able to strike the right balance.

"How can you be feminine if you are the boss?" asks Connie who feels that this dichotomy may be even more pronounced in Hong Kong in the Chinese culture. Even though women are stepping up all over, still many of them don't have the confidence to speak up in meetings, let alone be the boss.

"Guys instead are more forthcoming, when in fact the women are just as smart" notes Connie, pointing out the importance of having role models. As much as possible she tries to speak a lot at internal meetings and present on various issues. "It's important to be seen as someone who can show them a style," she says, "because there isn't enough visibility of senior women for junior women to have enough reference points."

Connie also encourages her team to be supportive of one another. So if a team member can't be available between 4 and 6pm to take care of his or her child, it's okay as long as they log back in after 6pm and look at some work.

"I encourage people to take control of their environment, relationships, clients and co-workers," she says meaning that it's important to be clear and constructive in communicating with different people. "You don't have to be some crazy dragon woman and shoot at people to get your point across." At one point, when she was younger Connie was criticized for being a bit of a cream puff because she was too nice. But actually she knew her clients loved her, and didn't let the comments interfere with her way of dealing with things.

### 24/7 Lifestyle

One of the biggest challenges today, for men and for women is keeping up with the 24/7 lifestyle, particularly in Hong Kong where the local time zone places us in a position between Europe and America that is conductive to joining a conference call at 11pm or early in the morning, a very common practice. Comparatively speaking, nobody would expect anyone in Australia to be awake and on a call at 11pm. To top it off, the zealous working culture in Hong Kong translates to really long working hours. And let's not forget technology. As much as the Blackberry has freed people from their desks, it now imposes a new kind of slavery in the expectation of quick replies.

"If you put all these things together, it means that having a sustainable career in Hong Kong is getting harder and harder," says Connie. "I don't know if people are going to be able to say I had a 25-year career in the future. Certainly it's going to be hard to follow the model I've followed, where I've been a lawyer for 25 years. I know I'm working harder now than I have ever had to before, despite being as senior as I am."

### What Companies Can Do

Because the biological and cultural issues for women aren't going to evaporate overnight, the first big step is to talk about the issues openly. The more people talk about the challenges, the more people can understand it is okay to have certain conversations. Mentoring for women is particularly important. As part of the company's female leadership program, Connie has been assigned an executive coach of her own, which she says has been very helpful.

Connie envisions that, the more senior women there are, the greater the inherent understanding of the difficulties younger women face. But lately there are a lot of senior men who have teenage daughters and they are starting to think about these issues for the first time. This reasoning did not apply to their wives who may have been at law school but decided to stop their careers. Now because suddenly they have a precious girl who is going off to university, they think, "What's going to happen to my daughter? Is she going to have a career?"

"For my part I know I can't change the world, but I always say to myself, 'Influence what you can influence'," says Connie. "So rather than thinking big I sometimes tell myself, 'Think small.'" For example Connie will extend a hand of friendship to a number of women in her firm in the same way that men forge ties with other men.

One of her top pointers for women is to not put their life on hold for anybody because if there's something they want to do, they don't want to regret it later on if it didn't happen.

At the moment Connie is mentoring a woman in her company who recently had twins. She tries to give her as much support as she can and she is actively encouraging her to do certain things while sharing her insight. So far the woman has done an amazing job juggling everything under the watchful eyes of her colleagues who acknowledge how hard it must be.

"I hope that little bit of encouragement and validation can help her decide whether to stick with the job or not. I don't know what else I could be doing," says Connie who sees the other side of the coin too. When things get stressful at home, sometimes coming back to work is a welcome relief as it makes one feel like she is good at something.

Connie's team is split equally between men and women, yet none of the women have senior roles yet. In 11 years as a partner in Hong Kong she's seen some wonderful women leave, so it's paramount to encourage women to stay in the workforce.

"At the end of the day most people want to have a relationship and possibly a family," Connie says. "Nobody wants to wake up at 40 in a flat alone, which means you need to make time. So how do we balance that almost primal desire with all of the complexity of the modern work environment? I don't think I have any particularly good insights other than how you deal with each other on an individual level," she says.

First you get people talking about the issues, then you can influence their values and finally you can influence behaviors.

And one last point to consider is that when women get involved in decision-making, they bring more balance and different perspectives to the table. A lot of people have wondered if the Lehman Brothers collapse could have been averted if there had been a few more women on that board. We'll never know. But what we can be certain of is that women are nurturing and they evaluate the effects on others, demonstrating classic and vital feminine traits that are more valuable than ever.

# Chapter 13 Equality Angelina Kwan

*She refused an offer from a tier one firm because of its unfairness, and instead joined a no-brand, interesting, and risky project of restructuring a bankrupt trading firm. A restless worker and a risk taker, she is passionate about helping women fight for **EQUALITY** and stand their ground.*

As you speed on the highway towards Central, it's impossible to miss the golden Far East Finance Centre in the enviably situated locale of Admiralty. Its exposed rusted edges hint at a past glory as does the usurpation of its front row standing by a new generation of buildings sprouting from the latest land reclamation site. That's life in Hong Kong. But if your office sits high enough in the building, the view is superb, second to none. That's the case with Angelina's office overlooking the whole fragrant harbor. And the inside of the office mirrors the breathtaking panorama, having just undergone a full makeover, its sleek furnishing still half-hidden in plastic wrap.

Towering over us by a couple of feet Angelina animatedly walks us around the refurbished facilities and talks us through her latest endeavors. She recently set up a consulting business to take on this project: the restructuring of a listed local trading firm that had gone bust, which she's doing by eviscerating it inside out. Overworked by a zillion responsibilities, right now she is like the building we stand in: running on reserve fuel. Yet she has agreed to meet us, knowing that her story has the potential to empower other women.

### A Brave Decision

Not long ago Angelina was unhappily employed in a big financial services firm. So she did what most people in her situation do: she started to look around. A major American company in her field was setting up office in Hong Kong so she thought to give it a go. She was flown business-class to New York for an exhausting round of interviews. After meeting 29 people, only one of whom was a woman, Angelina asked the CFO why they had such a sparse, or rather non-existent, female representation on the board and among seniors. He replied that they were in the process of changing this and hadn't had any success yet. He added that his wife was on his case about the paucity, too.

Satisfied by an honest answer and pleased by the general good vibes and professionalism, Angelina returned to Hong Kong, looking forward to receive the firm's proposal. It didn't take long to arrive. As she reviewed the terms of engagement, her eye fell on the compensation part: their offer was in the vicinity of what she got paid ten years earlier.

At first she thought it was a mistake and didn't react, but by the next morning, blood was boiling in her veins. This was not a mistake. They had seen her current contract and salary, they had checked her stellar list of references, they had all they needed to make an informed decision and this was the best offer they could think of?

"You've got to be kidding," recalls Angelina, still annoyed by the dubious proposition. That morning she called up the headhunter asking whether her package reflected the fact that she would have been the first Chinese and first senior woman the company hired. She emphasized: "Is this how you want to insult me?"

"No, no, no, no, no," quickly denied the headhunter. There must have been some kind of mistake.

That night over the phone Angelina confronted the CFO with the same verve: "Is it because you are all white males that you offered me this salary?" The man, unhappy about the racist and sexist accusation, having himself a Thai wife, conceded there was a mistake on their part and reassured Angelina that in the coming few hours she'd get a new contract matching the appropriate amount she was expecting.

"In fairness, they gave me back a contract with what I had been expecting, that reflected the position and my stature, and what I would have moved for if they had they done it the right way, but they didn't," she says thinking back.

Unsure about what to do, she sat on the new contract for a week. The more she thought about it the more she felt that she had been unfairly treated. Finally, she called the CFO to inform him that she couldn't accept. It had been too much of an insult and it would take a lot to reverse that. She reminded him that the company still had no women on their board nor had they a policy of hiring women. He replied she would have been the first to make that change. Angelina decided not to take the job.

Since then, the company has hired a handful of very good female traders in Hong Kong, which Angelina points out, it shows they are trying. She even sent them a sincere note to praise their increased progressive attitude.

But at the time of writing, they still didn't have any women on their board.

"At least I know that I stood up for myself," says Angelina, one eye filled with pride.

### Hiring Women and Quotas

Around that same time, Angelina was approached with a different offer. A local trading company had gone bankrupt and wanted Angelina to turn the firm's fate around. They offered her the right price from the start and gave her 100% freedom to hire and do what she had to do. It was an irresistible offer. She accepted and set up a consulting company to immediately start the project.

When we meet Angelina, she is a few months into the resurrection of the firm. The office has been gutted inside out and now looks every bit as sleek as any big firms of its kind. As she proudly shows us around, she talks about her plans.

"The traders will sit here. Look there, we have all the latest technology. Oh and here is a full kitchen…" She's in the process of hiring, she explains. Naturally her eyes are set on adding a good number of women, particularly in senior positions. There need to be more women, she reiterates. There's no better way to encourage change than to let it trickle down from the top.

We agree that the best way to encourage a larger representation of women in top jobs is by allowing an organic growth, but not all firms have enlightened leaders who want to create a more equal gender distribution across all levels of the company. We ask Angelina for her opinion on the quota issue – forcing companies to have a determined percentage of women on boards.

"I guess I hold a moderate position on this" says Angelina. "I believe that if you are forced a fixed amount of women it's going to be lip service. That being said, as an ex-regulator – and this is something my boss always said and I never believed him until I joined the Securities and Futures Commission (SFC) – people won't do anything unless they are forced to do so." In fact she adds that the SFC would not be necessary if everybody followed rules and played fairly.

"I don't believe you should mandate an amount specifically for women, but I believe there should be diverse boards that should adhere to specific terms such as a six-year rule because boards need new views and values as a company grows. Now if it is 33% women, 10% Asian and 5% African-American, I don't think that's something that should be mandated but the principle should be there and people should follow the principles."

Her main concern is that by setting fixed numbers, companies risk ending up with women who are neither capable nor interested in contributing. For example, Angelina was recently asked to be on the board of a company dealing in a specialized area of aerospace.

"How many women know about aircraft defense and aerospace? Not many. So how many do you think would want to go on the board of a Chinese company that does this?"

Not only do they lack the knowledge necessary to do a good job, they probably wouldn't even be interested in learning more about that subject. Angelina, however, agreed to that position, having some experience in the field from when she audited defense and aerospace companies. So with Angelina's general knowledge of the industry and with the company wanting a female with a financial background on the board, they made a perfect match. And naturally she is the sole female director in the company.

## Equal Hours

We ask Angelina to name the attitude adjustments that can help women be more competitive. "If women plan to have long and successful careers, they can't expect to work less than their male counterparts," she replies candidly. Just recently, Angelina had such a conversation with a young man she used to work with. He's now in a different company working with a predominantly male team and she knows he works long hours because they often speak to each other at 11pm while they are both still in their respective offices. That day he asked Angelina for some advice regarding a complaint he had received from a young woman who said she was given too much work and that she wouldn't be able to get out of work at that rate.

"If she wants to be treated as an equal in terms her work, then she has to put in the hours just like the guys do," Angelina told him. Of course if you have a family and kids there are ways to balance things, and you might not even be in financial services to start with. But this woman was young, single and complaining that she couldn't leave earlier, while the rest of her team members were working until 11pm. So if you want to be taken seriously you have to work as late, if not later, than the rest of the people you work with.

Now it's also true that there can be adjustments, particularly in financial services there could be a better work-life balance. But the nature of the job is intense, so women should know from the start what to expect and decide if they are fit for such routines. Expectations must be adjusted from the very beginning. Angelina for example, doesn't have any children, so she's okay with late nights in the office, but women and men with families may not be as ready to make such sacrifices.

## How Can Companies Allow Flexibility?

Although we respect Angelina's opinion, we don't believe that committing to or expecting 24-hour working days is going to help women rise to leadership positions, especially those who have a family. We raise the point of flexibility with Angelina.

"Unfortunately there isn't a single answer for flexibility because it means different things to different people, different companies, different industries and that's partially why it's so hard to agree on a sole solution," says Angelina. The most obvious path is to gain flexible hours by working part-time. But as Deborah Kan mentioned early on, and Angelina agrees now, doing part-time well is challenging. You nearly always end up with either an unhappy employer or (as in most cases) a miserable employee who ends up working almost full time hours with part-time pay. But it can be done, says Angelina, citing the example of a friend who part-timed for years successfully thanks to her strict discipline.

Angelina's friend had been the senior director for a major financial company for many years when she decided to leave her high position to work part-time in a law firm in order to make time for her kids and family. She was incredibly determined to make this work that while she was at work she was so productive – to the point that her output was nearly that of a full-time job - while only working part-time hours. When her kids left for college, she then returned to a full-time role and was immediately hired as the general counsel of another main financial firm in Hong Kong. Now it all sounds easy, but it had been a difficult decision for her.

When she first decided to leave her job she was just one step shy of becoming the executive director of that company. Yet she left because family life was really important to her. This shows that if you are focused and know what your priorities are, you can accomplish almost anything. This woman surely had a long-term plan and kept one foot in the financial world by networking and keeping connections alive, while manifesting an admirable work ethic, to ensure a smoother return later on. Yet getting paid half a salary to do a full-time job just because one is more efficient and is able to reduce the face-time hours spent in the office by half while doing the same amount of work doesn't seem particularly enticing, let alone fair, to us.

**Women's Reluctance to Talk About Business With Each Other**

"There should be something such as an old girls' network", says Angelina, but sadly women aren't good at helping each other out professionally. We agree with Angelina's view on this. There are many women's organizations out there, but they seem mostly concerned with organizing charity events than with providing real professional growth and networking opportunities for women with the aim of expanding professional opportunities. Women have a hard time talking to one another.

Guys instead excel at helping each other out as long as there isn't any conflict of interest. They meet at a club, have a drink, talk about work, then maybe an opportunity arises and they turn and say, 'Hey, are you interested?'

Women are so protective of their areas they are unlikely to introduce others to new jobs or even better jobs. Networking is crucial in this sense. It's a behavior that leaves Angelina perplexed. "Maybe they feel threatened?" she asks. Maybe they don't really talk about work when they meet, preferring more personal topics. Whatever the reason, it has to change.

The authors' view on the reluctance of women to talk about business with each other is that women tend to divide their relationships between 'personal' and 'business' relationships, not realizing that – especially by the time they have reached senior positions – often their friends are the same people they do business with. It is often said that men are unable to talk about personal problems with each other and therefore they end up talking about business when they meet, while women form deeper relationships because they discuss their private issues.

Most women, however, don't realize that, while it is often invaluable to be able to rely on women friends in troubled time, when they spend their whole time discussing their intimate relationships and personal issues they create two problems for themselves: (a) they waste a valuable opportunity to strengthen their business knowledge and network by exchanging business ideas and information with their friend, like men do on a constant basis; and (b) their friend will only remember them as a person they discuss personal issues with, and therefore will not think of putting them forward for a new role or consulting position when there is a chance to do so. They very likely involve someone who they only know on a professional basis. That's because the private conversations will have created a smoke screen around the woman's professional skills.

Angelina returns to the conversation she had with a young guy who had received the complaint from a young female colleague. When he was still working for her, one day he came to ask what he should do with his life, because he felt he wasn't learning in that job anymore. Angelina recalls, "I could have said, 'You've done so well here, we'll promote you,' but instead I told him that his skills in this division were non-transferable so he would not be able to use them outside. I suggested that if he wanted I could talk to somebody and move him to corporate finance. So basically I was willing to give up one of my best pawns for his career development. I think women need to help each other like that."

**Taking Risks and Getting Out of Your Comfort Zone**

The problem is also that women tend to get comfortable in their area and they aren't confident to do another job. Essentially they narrow their focus and accept the narrowing. As we've seen with most women in these stories, by taking risks they increased opportunities for themselves. Even women without kids end up getting pigeonholed.

"In my previous job I was very comfortable, people were nice and I got a lot of speaking engagements, but if you aren't happy and if the company doesn't take you seriously, then what's the purpose of you being there?" asks Angelina. "Just sit there in mediocrity? I just felt I wasn't making a change and I don't like to see things not pushed forward." She adds that, on the other hand, it's okay to not share her ambition, but then those women shouldn't complain about their jobs. If you want new chances, you have to go out and search for them.

We are reminded of the extraordinary Christine Loh. She wasn't happy in LegCo, feeling that she was not really contributing, so what does she do? She elopes and sets up the think tank. Surely her financial returns aren't as high but she made a decision.

"Same with me," says Angelina. "I left my position as the COO of a high-profile company to pick up this firm. It's a complete downer in terms of status." Just imagine that not long ago she was approached by some conference organizers asking her to speak at an event. When she told them she had left the big-shot company but that she'd still be happy to speak on that topic, they disappeared.

Angelina is obviously not scared of taking risks, with her motto being: "No risk, no return." She stresses the need to do things out of your comfort zone if you don't want to regret not doing things and complain about stagnating.

**Getting Personal**

"As I child I was always told, I was really stupid," says Angelina of a very Chinese parenting strategy. Her parents never failed to remind her that she wasn't as good as her siblings. Not surprisingly, the young Angelina cringed and felt somewhat lost. When she graduated from college she decided to go into accounting, instead of becoming a doctor which was what she had originally intended to do. She set her mind to be an accountant and to be good at it.

"Accounting is probably one of the most boring jobs on earth, but it's a stepping stone to becoming a professional," says Angelina who joined KPMG upon getting qualified. At that time she noticed vacancies in compliance and corporate governance, areas that in 1986 were just springing and becoming important. She quickly moved into areas where people hadn't yet moved into, and that really paid off when she came to Hong Kong.

In Los Angeles work is good if you are in banking, real estate or the entertainment industry, all of which have a glass ceiling for women. Although today it's slightly better, in 1986 when Angelina was just starting out, it was very hard for an Asian woman to get a senior role anywhere. So for her career and her happiness she decided to move to Hong Kong where all her closest friends were living.

She took a job at a financial services firm without knowing much about it, not knowing that her new boss would unleash a whole new world in front of her. She was in the right place at the right time. From the start he opened his rolodex and introduced her to everybody in town, saying he had a new head of internal audit who needed to learn quickly.

"He really mentored me in that sense and allowed me to go meet the head of the Futures Exchange, Stock Exchange and others. Within a few months I learned how systems worked in Hong Kong," She says.

In an attempt to return the mentoring she was given early in her career, Angelina tries to do the same with her staff now. She says she regularly invites them to join her at cocktail parties to work the circuit and introduce them around. But not a lot of people are up to it.

It's important as a young employee to notice when your boss is willing to mentor you. And even if you don't see the long-term importance of certain things at that moment, if you are planning on having a great career, you must trust your boss, get out of your comfort zone and network.

**The Power of a Group**

It was during this time that the Compliance Officers Group started to fill a gap in the system where general counsels had regular access to regulators but compliance professionals were often left behind.

"I called all the compliance officers from every firm I could find and at the beginning they were only eight people who met with a regulator on a monthly basis but shortly the group ballooned to 300 people meeting on a regular basis and this was before people could co-ordinate events via internet," Angelina says. Her boss loved the initiative. At these meetings they could discuss both regulatory and management issues. It was also a very powerful networking opportunity.

"A lot of people found jobs through that network," says Angelina, who also points out that interestingly the participation was split equally between men and women. For her too it turned out to be an opportunity to get close to the regulators. A real industry for compliance and corporate governance grew from that so when she started a compliance and legal department for another company because of all her contacts and relationships with all the regulators, she joined the Futures and Securities Commission and within it, she started making contacts with global regulators. This boosted her profile to a whole new dimension, as did the fact that her boss at the time encouraged her to go out and do speeches and travel in his place. She ended up staying there for eight years.

In hindsight, Angelina's breakthrough moment probably came when she started the compliance group because that allowed her to meet lots of people, but it also gave her the confidence to act on her own instincts. She wasn't forced to set up the support group, but she had a creative idea and she went for it. It would have been much easier for the young woman to use her free time to unwind and hang out with her friends. From that experience she also learned more about herself. She realized she was passionate about educating and helping people, whether it was with her group back then or helping women boost their careers today.

"It's fun to me and it's great to work with people who get things done. I even wrote the fund manager code of conduct which is still used today, and we were very proud of it."

The funny thing is that Angelina didn't set out with a master plan to become a hot shot. She was nowhere close to that, instead bumbling from one thing to another. Nothing had been designed, which is probably the best thing that could happen to her because ultimately it allowed her to always follow her passion and instincts.

"You must live like that," insists Angelina. "If not, nothing happens to you." She pauses for a moment to consider her next reflection. "But I tell you, I really thought I was going to go to that firm after nearly 30 interviews," she says, recalling the first story she shared with us. "I guess everything happens for a reason. This door opened at the same time, and with two interviews it was done!" Sometimes it's that easy, if you are willing to take risks.

# Chapter 14
# Support
# Teresa Ko

*If Teresa Ko had a magic wand, she would make sure all women had supportive environments to push them closer to their professional dreams. Without the* ***SUPPORT*** *of her family and friends, Teresa may have never become Freshfields' first-ever China Chairman, juggling some of the world's largest IPOs and a family at home.*

"No way, I'm not going to do this!" exclaimed Teresa 20 years ago, putting down the iron at once. That day was the first and last time she ironed her husband's shirts, six of them in all. As a young female lawyer in London working long hours and monotonously commuting on the tube morning and night, her last wish was to come home to a pile of laundry. With that, she and her nice understanding husband struck a deal: they would each iron their own clothes.

Upon hearing this, Teresa's mother told her newly married daughter, that there were ways around this domestic conundrum. She mentioned the popularity of domestic helpers in Hong Kong, hoping perhaps to lure her daughter back home after over a decade in the UK.

But it didn't take much to convince Teresa. The thought of being relieved of all domestic responsibilities was enough.

"Joking aside, it was a tremendous opportunity that Asia was holding out and Hong Kong had another 10 years before the handover so we decided to come back," says Teresa of the real motive behind their return to Hong Kong. Her firm in London didn't have a Hong Kong office so she had to find a new job. Freshfields, a small firm with only three partners and five associates was hiring and Teresa got the job.

Today Freshfields is one of the biggest practices in the world with over 280 employees just in Hong Kong. "I think I was at the right place at the right time, and was lucky to join a firm which was expansive in outlook," she says. Teresa also praises the firm's core values of nurturing talent and fairness - never once did she feel she was being discriminated against over the years.

Combine that opportunity at work with the terrific domestic support at a reasonable cost at home, both Teresa's career and family life flourished.

### Mandarin Cramming

In the early years of her career, Teresa was involved in various aspects of the legal business, from aircraft financing to a mixture of corporate work. Then her big break came in 1992. China had decided to list some of its state-owned enterprises on overseas exchanges such as Hong Kong's. Many law firms, including Freshfields, were invited to give seminars in China on how to do the listings, so a partner in the firm told Teresa this was going to be her job because it had to be done in Mandarin. She accepted but added that there was a problem: she could hardly speak the language.

"No problem," replied the partner. "You will be fluent in three weeks!"

In fits of panic, Teresa rang up her tutor. In the meantime, the speech was prepared in London and was externally translated, but when the mandarin tutor looked at the Chinese copy she couldn't understand a word of it. So, together, Teresa and her tutor painstakingly tweaked it word by word into colloquial Mandarin. Then for the remaining weeks Teresa recited it day in and day out as if she was singing an operetta.

The big day arrived. She rather enjoyed the experience as she felt the audience sat up and listened and soon after that Freshfields landed a mandate to work on what is now Sinopec Shanghai Petrochemical, the first state-owned enterprise to be listed both on the Hong Kong stock exchange and the New York stock exchange. At that time, the Chinese government approved nine companies to be listed in Hong Kong. Excited by having successfully completed a landmark listing, Teresa told the then-senior partner that having done one listing looked like an accident but to be able to do two meant that they would have a track record, so they should go for another one. He agreed and suggested that she get that second one too. Today, Teresa is a leader in Hong Kong capital markets work and has advised on the world's largest IPOs.

**Passion and Support**

To spend this much time at work can only mean that she enjoys it very much. We ask her if it's true. From the corner of the room the firm's business development manager, Jennifer, nods.

"Yes, I don't think I've found anything else just as fun," agrees Teresa. Naturally at her level, she has a lot of opportunities to influence others and she recognizes that responsibility. At the moment she is increasingly asking herself how she can make an impact on the things she does on a day-to-day basis. It could be a small gesture or doing something with the power of inspiring somebody else.

"I think it's sometimes hard to push all the responsibility onto the woman because in my view all the stars have to be aligned," says Teresa. Women may be full of passion and ambition, but here in Asia and particularly in Hong Kong, if her entourage is not supportive and encouraging it is very hard for her to make it professionally. For example, if your boyfriend thinks you shouldn't be working this hard, or your parents think you should focus on getting married rather than giving presentations, then how can you give your best at work? Peer pressure could come from friends too, if they think you aren't making the most of your career and you should perhaps go to a place where you can work more regular hours. It's easy to get worn down by the everyday detractors.

One way, notes Teresa, would be for the woman to influence the people around her so that she can strike more of a balance, but it takes a very determined woman who isn't afraid of going against the current and taking risks.

On the other hand, we must be aware that if there's a place in the world where women are more likely to succeed in their career and try to "have it all" it is Hong Kong because of the widely available domestic support and reasonably priced childcare.

### What Companies Can Do

"There are companies that think that women can advance if they behave more like men, but it would be a sad world if that was the only way to seek advancement. I'm not of that school at all. I think there are a lot of strengths in our femininity," says Teresa, pointing out women can be tough negotiators but at the same time they have a softer side which can be useful in mediation, particularly to bridge the gap between two strong opposing positions.

According to Teresa what companies need to do is to be conscious of women's roles outside of work. For example, during transactions at the office (and this applies to men too) it's vital to work with a team and focus on teamwork. So, if someone has an important engagement, such as the girlfriend or boyfriend's birthday or a dinner for the mother-in-law's 60$^{th}$ birthday, then there is someone in the team to cover for that person. At some point, and more often than not, everyone, whether they happen to be a parent or not, will have some kind of personal commitment. Accordingly, the organization needs to understand these needs and find ways to support them. Companies need to embrace that basic awareness that people have responsibilities outside of the office, and once we have that understanding in relation to important commitments and personal priorities it will trickle down to just achieving an everyday balance, which is very important.

Up to now many companies have been reticent to bring about this change because they simply don't see advantages in doing that or they can't be bothered. But things are shifting, slowly. Companies are starting to value staff that is happy and engaged which in turn leads to higher staff retention.

Teresa asks: "Does the employee treat work as just a job? Or is it a place where they want to be to develop themselves, develop their skills and themselves at a personal level to be better than they have been, to challenge themselves and to tackle things that they have never considered being capable of doing?"

If you analyze what makes a person happy in the workplace, there are lots of elements: being respected, being able to learn, but managing their stresses and pressures outside of work is also very much part of it. If employees feel like they have kids at home and no one is looking after them properly, they can't possibly be happy in the office. So it's really a holistic thing and it doesn't necessarily have to be a mother with kids. It could be somebody who has not been lucky to find the right special someone, which is tough in Hong Kong.

"I'm not advocating that firms have to be dating agencies, but I have been known to have organized a 'speed-dating game' at one of our off sites which was very well-received," says Teresa with a little smirk. Boys and girls sat facing each other. They had three questions each, and one minute before moving to the next 'date'. The first two questions were: "Which university did you go to" and "In which office do you work and in what area?" which were instrumental to gain basic knowledge of each other and the third question was free. To everybody's amazement there was a lot of: "Are you going out with anyone?"

"That was very funny! Some of them still talk about it to this day. It was my attempt to try and integrate our associates in our three offices in China so that they could get to know each other more quickly because if we rely on them to break the ice and get around to everybody it will take too long," explains Teresa.

**Work-Life Balance**

More than men, women really need to integrate life with work and they are increasingly aware of that need. Sometimes all it takes is a readjusting of hours and strictly adhering to them, but with Blackberries keeping you connected all the time and everywhere it can be challenging to switch off work mode.

Teresa admits that's an ongoing challenge for her, so she needs to be very conscious about giving herself and the people at home quality time to engage and to communicate. "It's a balance that's easier said than done," she says.

Once you switch off your email and phone calls, to be able to fully make the most of personal time, Teresa believes it's necessary to be good at organizing the scheduling of your time so that you can fit in as much as possible.

"Sometimes it works and sometimes it doesn't: could I do with more downtime? Yes, of course, a lot more! But do I work so hard that there is no life? No, I don't, but you have to have people who are very supportive around you. My children have practically worked around my schedule which, in an ideal world should it be like that? No, it shouldn't, so no doubt there have to be sacrifices, it's the same way men sacrifice. They travel in and travel out and just stay home on weekends; in some cases it's even more extreme, than what you see in women."

During the life cycle of a child, there are stages when you can work more and stages when you have to work less. Reluctantly admitting this, Teresa says that her approach has been that with an infant you can be less involved because so long as they are being taken care of, properly fed and given a comfortable environment and the care is good quality, that's fine. Of course, it's necessary to have bonding time, but it's not as if you have to sit at home and stare at the baby while he sleeps – "which I have done!" adds Teresa. Then when they become a toddler, that's the fun part and you don't want to miss too much of it, but at the same time you grow tired of it because you chase after them all day. So, at different stages of a child's development, there are different ways of connecting and spending time.

"I now have a 14- and 17-year-old and that is really when you need to spend much more time with them," she says. "I think you have to seize every moment and make the most out of it. It's all about organizing your time, anticipating and planning in advance and being hugely efficient."

Ultimately, for women like Teresa, it's about the quality of the time you spend together rather than the quantity. Ironically there are many parents with far less demanding jobs and a lot more free time, but they choose not to engage their children as much, because it's so much easier to not organize anything and let the children entertain themselves in front of an iPad or the TV. Good parenting is the same for working parents as well as stay-at-home parents; it means that the exchange between parent and child allows the parent to be more up-to-date with everything that's going on with the younger generation and the child to be imbued with important values from the parent.

**Guilt**

Teresa feels that while one has to be very conscious and work at finding more time every day to be with the people who are important and achieve a balance – which may mean different things to different people – feeling guilty is not the way to do it. Guilt is just a waste of your energies.

Countless working mothers are torn apart by the guilt of not spending enough time with their children. At times it is so pronounced that it alone can be the motive to stop them from working or spending too much time and energy at work. Unlike these women, Teresa thinks it's negative to feel guilty. Instead she suggests using that guilt energy towards finding ways to remedy a situation.

"If you feel guilty, then don't go to work," justly points out Teresa. "It would be pointless to work and be a parent half-heartedly because most of your energy is eaten away by guilt. That way, you end up doing nothing well".

From the back of the room, Jennifer points out: "One thing Teresa is good at it is being very much in the moment. If she's here, then she's all here – you don't get half-way – you get someone who's focused on what's going on." We absolutely agree. Getting Teresa to sit here in front of us had been agonizing, having to postpone our date multiple times over three months. We had nearly lost hope that we could meet her. But as we sit across from Teresa today, we happily get her full attention and a super-engaging, candid account.

However, we refuse to let the guilt issue fall so easily. If it were that easy to deal with guilt, not as many women would be struggling with it. So we press her on the topic.

"You have to work at it," says Teresa. For example, since her daughter is now studying in England, every time her business schedule allows it, she will go meet her to spend the weekend together. Whether it is for a day or the whole weekend, she will then consciously put away her Blackberry for chunks of time and try hard to make something out of the weekend by planning activities in advance.

"We are now very good at planning holidays and we enjoy the planning bit too, but there are disappointments. I had hoped to take her to Peru to see Machu Picchu this summer, whilst my husband took my son to Canada with some of his friends. But obviously at work we are going through a very busy patch so there's just no way that I can be away for 10 days with no access to the mobile or GPRS. I had to cancel our trip. In place of that we went to Bangkok for a weekend of shopping and just milling around the market. It was nice, but I know I would have loved to do the other trip with her. So you have to manage it. In my entire life I have never told them where we would go on holiday until practically two days beforehand when they were young, so as not to result in disappointment...it's something you just have to live with, I guess…"

For Teresa, being brilliant at work also means being a great role model to one's children, particularly when the children are old enough to understand the importance of hard work and self-fulfillment. But Teresa warns that striving towards can sometimes pose challenges. Her daughter recently drew for her a wonderful invitation card that she thought was out of this world, but her daughter kept saying it was not good enough.

"She has very high standards so it's important to manage that because you don't want to raise kids who are never satisfied with what they do because they always think they can do something much better."

To conclude, we ask Teresa what she would do if she had a magic wand and immediately change something which would boost women's opportunities. "I think I would like the people around women to say 'go for it!' It is so important for other people to say it and be positively encouraging instead of saying, you decide".

Teresa talks at length on the importance of support from others, so we ask her whether she has had a lot of support herself. She replies softly "Well, yes, I'm very lucky".

Teresa is busy, but she still finds time to pursue her own interests. Having lived in England throughout most of her formative years, she has been very much influenced by an essentially British tradition (or could it be the Chinese one?) – drinking tea.

At the moment she's looking at antique silver teapots on the internet and she is planning a wonderful tea party to share her favorite pastime with colleagues and friends.

She also finds walking relaxing. “It is the safest form of exercise: sunrise and sunsets are all free,” she says “and wonderful”. We agree with her.

# Chapter 15
# Power
# Rachel Huf

*When the conditions are right, women working together towards a unified goal have the **POWER** to change anything – even what before might have seemed impossible. Rachel Huf and a group of women at Barclays did just that.*

In 2006, senior management at Barclays, led by the CEO and head of HR, gathered a group of senior women and asked them to form a women's group. It was not unusual for an investment bank to set up such an initiative. Most large organizations have some kind of women's internal network, but despite the good intentions to impact women's careers, it is unusual that anything substantial ever results from their initiatives. This was not the case at Barclays.

With absolute backing from the top executives - who were all male – the women of Barclays were given *tabula rasa*. They could take this group in whichever direction they wished, and all they had to do was present a plan to the executives who would support them and try to get them a budget.

"So we got together and thought, 'What do we really want to do?'" says Rachel Huf, Managing Director, Legal at Barclays Capital who was part of the steering committee called the *Women's Initiatives Network*. They decided that they wanted their first initiative to be something that made a difference for Barclays' employees across Asia. They all agreed that one of the biggest challenges as a working mother in this part of the world were the terrible maternity leave policies, disparate from one country to the other.

In each jurisdiction, Barclays followed the statutory requirements so for Hong Kong that was ten weeks. The women thought it would be a great and useful change to have a consistent and competitive maternity policy for Barclays across Asia.

To come up with a fair yet advantageous package, the ladies considered the policy at their London headquarters, where women were entitled up to a year of maternity leave. That was fantastic. Then they looked around Asia and compared themselves to their peers in other investment banks and law firms and benchmarked themselves against them. There was a whole range: from companies that had the minimum eight weeks, to the best that had four months of paid leave.

"We'd like to better that!" thought the ladies. They proposed five months paid maternity leave throughout Asia. Senior management and HR kept their word, and eventually some months later, after some convincing, approved the policy. The new policy was a real coup for the bank, a definite improvement for working mothers, and a great marketing story, showing that Barclays is behind women's issues and cares about work-life balance.

"The funny thing is that I was one of the first people to take advantage of this!" says Rachel who together with another lady from the steering committee became pregnant before the new policy was announced. And the trend didn't stop. In the legal department where 68% are women, this new package made a huge impact.

A number of women have had two children at Barclays and one is about to have her third, but most of all the move seems to be a great retention tool. A number of people have stayed with the company for six years or more, which in Hong Kong, where people tend to change jobs every two to three years, is quite an achievement.

"It's great to be able to retain people and give them the flexibility they need to spend some time out their families and then come back to Barclays," says Rachel.

It took a group of confident women to push this forward. But Rachel hadn't always been this confident. When she had her first child she was working at Deutsche Bank. The company adhered to the classic minimum ten-week maternity policy, but Rachel wanted to spend more time with her newborn and requested four months leave.

"I was a bit nervous about it actually," says the lawyer, uncertain of how her standing in the company might change during her absence. Coincidentally, just as she was about to go on maternity leave, another company rang her about a job. In doubt about what might happen in the near future, she told them that she was about to give birth, but that if they still had an opening a few months later, they should consider her. Around that time, a good friend who had already had two children heartened her by telling her that four months in the course of one's career is nothing.

"She said I should not worry" says Rachel. "That I was entitled to maternity leave and once I got back I would carry on from where I left off. But what was really motivating was that while I was on maternity leave I got promoted!" Now that's something that gives you confidence.

## Looking at The Future

These days Rachel is starting to ponder what other changes might improve her work-life balance in this stage of her life. Having more time is definitely a priority, especially now that her children are older and need help with homework. But she is still thinking of the best way to achieve more balance while progressing in her career. Different solutions seem possible. A colleague in her legal team has recently started working a four-day week.

"It is the first experience we have of someone working flexi-hours and so far it's working well," says Rachel, adding that it's not something that is necessarily going to work for every position in an investment banking environment. Another friend who works in a different bank, every year takes an additional month off so she can spend more time with the children around summer holidays.

But again, it is not quite the solution Rachel is after. "For me, I would just like to have more flexible time, to be able to leave the office at a certain time so that I can take care of business at home and then ring back to the office when I need to," says Rachel. In Hong Kong this is really challenging because the international working style requires a 24/7 availability to work with London, New York and Australia. Invariably there are going to be calls and obligations at night. What's more, because Hong Kong is known for being so efficient, there is always the expectation that everything should be answered and addressed immediately. Of course smart phones make that possible, but they are a double-edged sword: on the one hand you are freed from sitting at your desk, but on the other you need to reply promptly.

While the *Women's Initiatives Network* is still considering how to crack the flexibility issue, they have kept busy with other kinds of initiatives. They have a senior women leadership program, they do community outreach, and they are helping to build other diversity platforms. But perhaps the single most important thing that happens at Barclays is that senior managers are encouraged to champion a diversity issue and during appraisal every year they have to answer a question about how they have contributed to diversity.

"This element together with the extended maternity leave is a great advertisement for us when hiring new staff" says Rachel with a big smile. With such strong support from top management, there's no doubt the ladies at the *Women's Initiatives Network* will be rolling out other exciting changes soon.

# Conclusion

Sometimes more than their male counterparts, women have a need for balance. While men seem to walk through their lives in a straight line, women often have a stronger need to balance time and energies spent on different aspects of their life and carry the burden, as well as the joy, of having to integrate those different aspects.

Men tend to be directional achievers – they often have an objective, a vision, a purpose and they go for it wholeheartedly while managing other interests and family commitments on the side. In contrast, women in general tend to have a need for a rounder life, where all areas are included and all areas bring fulfillment: they need to consolidate professional ambition and purpose, personal fulfillment, nurturing, exploring, contribution and connection.

This is also due to the fact that women still hold the major emotional – as well as physical in terms of time spent - responsibility for relationships and family. If you have a boyfriend or husband and a family you know that is very much like running a small business.

Women really need to hold together a lot more in their lives and find a way to make it work. And this is very difficult.

When we are in our twenties and fresh out of university, we set goals, our career goals. We make plans. We get into our corporate offices and keep on walking in a straight line following those plans, as men do. Then we hit a road bump, usually around 34 years old up to 40. As we struggle to find the right balance between family and work, to coast through the hardships of being a new mother, we look around for role models and we don't find many. There are still very few role models of successful, balanced women at the top.

So what happens?

Some women drop out of their corporate career, thinking they will find satisfaction in family or other lifestyles. We have several very intelligent, highly qualified friends who resigned from their jobs and thought they would be happy raising their children, doing charity work, or becoming full-time yoga teachers. Although some of them are perfectly happy with their decision, many of them later regretted it. They regretted losing their financial independence, their presence in society, in other words their power.

Some start businesses and become successful and fulfilled entrepreneurs.

Those who continue in their corporate career, however, often feel unsatisfied and under unbearable pressure. They try to make everything work with their career, their relationships, their interests, their concern for the world. But they feel that nothing is working.

For this reason women often feel a sort of identity crisis, an inferiority complex, a preoccupation with unattainable perfection that leaves many of us feeling we do not measure up *enough*. It is difficult to feel like you are a good mother, because you can't compete with stay-at-home moms, and it is difficult to feel like a great professional, because you can't compete with the amount of time men spend in the office.

Women also worry about the contradictions between acceptable feminine behavior and the requirements of powerful positions.

It isn't lack of ambition or a desire to dedicate themselves full-time to family that drives women away from the corporate world in their mid-30s. Instead, it is mostly the difficulty in continuing to walk a straight line path that doesn't work anymore when family commitments and personal development need to find their place in a busy life.

Leadership is often not something you are born with – leadership is something you develop along the way, and therefore the first step to leadership is to take care of ourselves. At the same time, it is true that without a clear support system in organizations that allows women to thrive throughout the early years of motherhood and to integrate the all-round life they crave, we are not going very far.

Women who have been able to tread the path of leadership have found ways to integrate their life: their personality, passions, technical knowledge, and femininity are all intertwined with their professional life – not separated from it. Those who have families have been smart about creating around them an environment that supports them during those difficult years of early child-rearing when they need to make an extra effort to balance personal and professional responsibilities. All of them have learned to boldly seek opportunities and demand promotions without undermining their femininity and core values.

These women often don't separate life and work in a surgical manner. All of them have a strong passion for what they do and how they do it, and at the same time all of them are able integrate their life and work in a particular way. All of them love what they do also because of the opportunities it gives them to influence the outside world, to make an impact, to have power to do things.

All of them have learned how to play by the rules but also how to break them, or bend them, to make space for their life and to fight for what they want. All the women we have interviewed in this book – with their different personalities and their own unique ways of dealing with challenges and opportunities – are torchbearers of a new generation of women who want to make a difference in their environment, both at home and at work if they have families.

In all of this, there remains the question of what corporations can do to create more opportunities for women.

Some companies, especially in European countries like Norway where women must comprise 40% of board seats, are implementing policies of having a minimum number of women in leadership positions. We know this is a controversial decision, and some women feel offended by it. Most of the women we have interviewed in this book have generally expressed moderate opinions about this point.

I used to be very conflicted about the quota issue. Initially, like many women, I saw it as a defeat, as a reverse discrimination. I am aware that there is a high percentage of highly successful women who have strong views against it.

However, after long consideration, I realized something. At the beginning of my career I was a telecommunications regulatory lawyer. My J.D. thesis was on the liberalization of the European telecommunications market, which was just happening at the time of my legal studies in the late nineties. Therefore during my first years as a lawyer I was heavily involved in helping new companies enter the telecommunications market, obtain licenses and negotiate interconnection contracts with the market incumbents (the former monopolists). Without regulation, the telecommunications market would have never been liberalized and those new players would have never had the strength and leverage to negotiate their positions. After a few years, when enough players and a solid free market system was in place, the market was deregulated. We would not have a free telecommunications market right now if it hadn't been for regulatory intervention, notwithstanding the fact that many of the new operators are better and more effective than the old monopolists.

I see women's situation as being very similar. It is a fact that women are not making it to top leadership positions because the rules by which business is run are men's rules. A regulatory intervention would open that gate for women; it would, in a sense, liberalize the market. We only need a quota to be in place for a few years, and then women will run on their own strength. Women at the top will serve as role models to younger women. They will help create the right infrastructures and a culture of real diversity. I am aware, however, that there are different opinions on this point.

Another point is the flexibility that companies are gradually implementing, through formal flexible policies or informal acceptance of employees working from home thanks to the technology means provided.

Women do not expect privileges per se, but they are aware of the necessity to ask for levels of flexibility if they have to compete in a man's world while at the same time remaining the primary caregiver at home.

Women also are starting to create movements to lobby for what they need. The example of what an internal women's network has been able to achieve at Barclays Capital – to change something important like maternity leave, is a clear step towards building an environment at work that formally supports family commitments, which in turn makes it possible for women to really give their best as professionals. Environments where a family-supportive culture is entrenched, like we heard from some of our interviewees, are also a fundamental enabler.

Finally, creating supportive environments at home is possibly the most important tool that successful women rely upon. A supportive significant other and family, reliance on quality domestic help and childcare education without guilt can make a huge difference.

So the issue as we see it isn't so much whether women can have it all, but rather how to integrate with a personality that can make the most of opportunities and in results-oriented, flexible, open-minded environments that leave room for an osmosis and natural flow between work and personal and family commitments. The goal is for each woman, in her own individual way, to be truly free to contribute her best resources.

## Other books by Stefania Lucchetti